T0317726

To the Brink of Destruction

A volume in the series

Cornell Studies in Money

Edited by Eric Helleiner and Jonathan Kirshner

A list of titles in this series is available at cornellpress.cornell.edu

To the Brink of Destruction

America's Rating Agencies and Financial Crisis

Timothy J. Sinclair

Cornell University Press

Ithaca and London

Copyright © 2021 by Cornell University

All rights reserved. Except for brief quotations in a review, this book, or
parts thereof, must not be reproduced in any form without permission
in writing from the publisher. For information, address Cornell University
Press, Sage House, 512 East State Street, Ithaca, New York 14850. Visit our
website at cornellpress.cornell.edu.

First published 2021 by Cornell University Press

Library of Congress Cataloging-in-Publication Data

Names: Sinclair, Timothy J., author.
Title: To the brink of destruction : America's rating agencies and financial
    crisis / Timothy J. Sinclair.
Description: Ithaca [New York] : Cornell University Press, 2021. |
    Series: Cornell studies in money | Includes bibliographical references
    and index.
Identifiers: LCCN 2020056479 (print) | LCCN 2020056480 (ebook) |
    ISBN 9781501760242 (hardcover) | ISBN 9781501760259 (ebook) |
    ISBN 9781501760266 (pdf)
Subjects: LCSH: Rating agencies (Finance)—United States. | Rating
    agencies (Finance)—United States—History—21st century. |
    Global Financial Crisis, 2008–2009. | Financial crises—United States
Classification: LCC HG3751.7 .S563 2021 (print) | LCC HG3751.7 (ebook) |
    DDC 332.1/78—dc23
LC record available at https://lccn.loc.gov/2020056479
LC ebook record available at https://lccn.loc.gov/2020056480

For Owen and Simon

Contents

Preface

The publication of this book is the most recent product of thirty years of thinking, talking, and writing about America's rating agencies. When I started this work, I did not appreciate the degree to which rating would become such a major feature of the global financial system. If the shift from traditional bank lending to capital markets is the long-run trend, as I think it is, then many judgments in our financial system will likely increasingly occur in the Big Three, comprising Moody's, S&P, and Fitch.

Most scholars have one opportunity to offer their views about some phenomenon that puzzles them. But to consider something over the long term, to observe change, to revise your thinking, is potentially a great benefit to understanding. Because I had the luck to investigate something that became increasingly important over time, and because these institutions have been involved in some of the most catastrophic events in financial markets and associated politics since the end of World War II, I hope readers will agree it made sense for me to write this new book on the agencies.

Working on this book happily took me back to New York City, staying at the now sadly defunct Larchmont Hotel on West 11th Street in the West Village. This time, I made extensive use of the Rose Main Reading Room at the New York Public Library at

Bryant Park. This served as a base for field work expeditions to the financial district and elsewhere. At the time, the library also provided a room for scholars, which I used for some of the meetings that informed this book.

Field work in New York, Paris, and London was supported by a British Academy/Leverhulme Small Research Grant, SG131031, for which I am thankful to the British Academy and Leverhulme Trust. Gary Fisher gave excellent advice on the application. Jackie Clarke helped make supporting funds available from the Department of Politics and International Studies at the University of Warwick. Jill Pavey helped me greatly in administering the grant.

At Moody's, I would like to thank Ryan Mensing, Janet Holmes, Nigel Phipps, and Nicola Fleming. At Standard & Poor's, I am most thankful to Catherine J. Mathis, Jayan Dhru, and James Wiemken for their time and insights. At Fitch, I was very lucky to meet with Ian Linnell in 2014 and 2020. Ian's executive assistant, Joanne Ridge Sims, arranged all this with professionalism and courtesy, despite the pandemic complicating matters. Jermone Fons, formerly of Moody's but then at Kroll Bond Rating Agency, talked to me at length. I met with Ann Rutledge of CreditSpectrum, also ex-Moody's, several times in New York, to my great benefit. Bill Harrington, yet another former Moody's staffer, shared his acute insights with me many times. I discussed some of the issues in this book with David Levey, who retired from Moody's as Managing Director and Co-head of the Sovereign ratings unit in 2005. David had a central role in creating Moody's country credit analysis methodology. As in the past, he was a font of insight and wisdom. In Paris, Raquel de Julian Artajo, Nadia El Gharbi, and Thierry Sessin-Caracci of ESMA (the European Securities and Markets Authority) kindly invited me to participate in a brown bag lunch at their offices.

I had long discussions with Bart Paudyn, Fumihito Gotoh, Giulia Mennillo, and Ginevra Marandola while thinking through some of the arguments made in this book. Bart visited the University of Warwick in 2011. Fumihito Gotoh, a former doctoral student of mine and now a colleague, who benefits from twenty-five years of credit research experience in Tokyo, wrote an article with me on rating in Japan. Dr. Gotoh also served as rapporteur at the workshop on the manuscript of this book held at the University of Warwick in January 2019. Giulia and I wrote an article on the regulation of rating. Dr. Mennillo's book on rating is an excellent introduction to the political economy of rating agencies. Dr. Marandola and I wrote a book chapter together that draws on some thoughtful parallels she developed between credit rating and the world of restaurant ratings. Ginevra, who visited Warwick in 2012/2013, during her doctoral studies at the University of Rome Tor Vergata, drew my attention to the repeal of a key feature of Dodd-Frank, which is discussed in this book. Tobias Hoffarth, a graduate student at the University of Warwick, was an effective research assistant, helping gather information on rating regulation.

My colleague Matthew Clayton helped me in what proved to be two very important ways. When I was wondering about what idiom to adopt, he gave me sage advice that has made the text of this book stronger, and I hope, more interesting to others. He also suggested I organize the manuscript workshop that took place at Warwick in January 2019.

The manuscript workshop, which examined the first draft over several hours, included comments and questions by Paul Langley (Durham), Peter Burnham (Birmingham), and a host of Warwick colleagues, including Ben Clift, Chris Clarke, Nina Boy, Johannes Petry, Fumihito Gotoh, Iain Pirie, Ruben Kremers, and Fabian

Pape. I must thank Paul for sharing his story about my driving. This event turned out to be a key step in the development of the book, and I thank everyone who participated in different ways. I recommend a manuscript workshop to other authors—provided, of course, they have a thick skin.

In addition to the various published papers I have authored and coauthored in recent years, the thinking presented in this book developed through public lectures and academic talks given at the Graduate Institute Geneva, the Financial Crises as Global Challenges symposium in Hannover, at Carleton University, the University of Leeds, the University of Erfurt, the Justus Liebig University Giessen, the University of York, Copenhagen Business School, the University of Birmingham, the University of Sheffield, and the University of Lund.

Tony Payne kindly made it possible for me to spend 2013/14 as a visiting scholar at the Sheffield Political Economy Research Institute at the University of Sheffield. I want to thank Koen Lamberts, the President and Vice-Chancellor of the University of Sheffield, whom I met when he worked at the University of Warwick, and Chris Hughes, Pro-Vice-Chancellor and formerly head of the Department of Politics and International Studies at Warwick. There is a good chance this book might never have been written without their encouragement and facilitation.

I want to thank Roger Haydon for being the most encouraging and exacting editor imaginable. I hope this book was a little easier for him than my first one. Roger, the leading social science editor of his time, retired from Cornell University Press just as I was making the finishing touches to the manuscript prior to it going into production. He made a huge difference to scholarship in the social sciences by nurturing several generations of young scholars. Roger's deep understanding and thoughtful guidance will be sorely missed. At the Press, I also want to thank Ellen Labbate, who prepared the manuscript for the editing and production departments, and Emily Andrew, who took over the Money series from Roger.

Eric Helleiner's gentle encouragement and pointed comments were also instrumental in the development of the text. I wish to also thank the anonymous peer reviewers and the editorial board, who could see what I was doing but gave me some useful ideas that have strengthened the book.

My son Henry and my spouse Nicole Lindstrom helped me in different ways. Henry made it clear there is more to life than writing books. They are no substitute for soccer, computer games, and bike rides. Following his advice, during the COVID-19 lockdown I purchased a bicycle and took my first ride since 1985. Nicole and I discussed some of the key issues investigated here, helping me make the manuscript stronger. For these things and much more I am very grateful to them both.

Owen F. Prior (b. 1928) and his son Simon D. Prior (1954–2013), my uncle and cousin respectively, were models of vocation and civic responsibility for me as I grew up in small-town New Zealand. The second and third generations in a family of physicians that now stretches to four, they brilliantly combined scientific understanding, compassion for others, humor, and a practical Kiwi approach to life. This book is dedicated to them.

TIMOTHY J. SINCLAIR
York, England

To the Brink of Destruction

1

Introduction

> The story of the credit rating agencies is a story of a colossal failure. The credit rating agencies occupy a special place in our financial markets. Millions of investors rely on them for independent objective assessments. The rating agencies broke this bond of trust . . . The result is that our entire financial system is now at risk.
> —*US Representative Henry A. Waxman, 2008*

Given the anger generated by the institutional failures and bail-outs that were features of the worst financial crisis since the 1930s, you might think many of the organizations involved must have ceased to exist, or at the very least been substantially reformed, making a repeat of the crisis impossible.

But you would be wrong. Yes, Bear Stearns has gone, and Lehman Brothers is, of course, no more. But, like Fannie Mae, the Federal National Mortgage Association, Freddie Mac, the Federal Home Loan Corporation, and most of the banks, the major American credit rating agencies are still there, at the heart of Wall Street and the global financial system, and they remain substantially unreformed. Despite being referred to as "essential cogs in the wheel of financial destruction," their business model is the same as it was before the crisis, and their analytical processes do not differ greatly from what they were years ago.[1] They have not been replaced by alternative systems, and what they do is as important today as it was before the crisis. Maybe more so.

Moody's Investors Service (Moody's), Standard & Poor's, currently branded as S&P Global Ratings (S&P), and Fitch Ratings (Fitch) have been at the center of the bond markets since the early years of the twentieth century. In recent decades the lower cost of debt financing in those markets challenged the traditional role of banks as corporate lenders, giving rise to the astonishing wave of financial innovation by the banks that helped create the global financial crisis beginning in 2007. The rating agencies played a significant role in this drama. Most people seem to believe the agencies simply inflated the ratings of bonds supported by housing debt, so they could be paid handsome fees by the issuers of those bonds. Understanding what the agencies really did, and why, and how they survived the ignominy of their involvement in the crisis is the purpose of this book.

Rating agencies are enigmas. Many think they can be understood using the same ideas and tools applied to banks and other financial institutions, but this has proven elusive. The agencies are not financial institutions. The core of their business is not a series of financial transactions on which they hope to show a profit. They do not provide financing, take deposits, or trade on their own account. The business of the agencies is looking into the future and offering a view of the likelihood of repayment by the issuers of bonds to potential investors. To do this, they must think about all the relevant circumstances, the capacity to repay by the issuers of

---

1. *The Financial Crisis Inquiry Report: Final Report of the National Commission on the Causes of the Financial and Economic Crisis in the United States* (New York: PublicAffairs, 2011), xxv.

the bonds, and their willingness to repay (as opposed to using those funds for some other purpose).

In selling their services the agencies are really selling confidence in themselves as experts about what is likely to happen in the future. This element makes all the difference because it means those who use ratings, even if those ratings prove not to be effective estimations of the future, can always suggest they were buying the best expertise available to them at the time. Contrast this with a financial transaction, where proof is in the bottom line.

Consequences

There is no doubt the events that began in 2007 were, short of military invasion, a pandemic like COVID-19 or famine, about as dramatic as it gets in the world of the twenty-first century. Banks failed, they were bailed out, and governments were indebted by bailing them out. It became very hard to borrow money even for the most creditworthy of potential borrowers in the months following the Lehman collapse on September 15, 2008. Governments considered all manner of possible responses to the situation. After two decades or more of globalization, here were Western governments rescuing the financial markets as had not happened since the 1930s.

The crisis generated considerable fear and hostility toward financial institutions, and for a time, perhaps in 2009 when world trade was at a low ebb, it seemed like systemic change was likely. Stimulus packages in China and the United States slowly revived world trade and growth. Efforts to consider what went wrong in the United States and in Europe did produce calls for wholesale change. But talk is cheap.

There was a good deal of questioning of the prevailing frameworks that guide policy and market institutions. But these ways of thinking proved remarkably resistant to criticism. This is not necessarily due to their merits, but because other ways of thinking about markets have been marginalized since the Thatcher and Reagan administrations in the 1980s. Rather than stimulating an intellectual revolution in how we view finance, coupled with the founding of new institutions and better conceived, more structurally sound market rules, the response to the crisis has largely consisted of an effort to slow down and contain finance, with the hope that these new burdens will somehow bring better financial behavior.

The rating agencies illustrate this response well. Many options were floated for the future of the agencies, including the establishment of a new international organization to undertake ratings, new business models, and new analytical models for the agencies. What we have seen instead is a reinvigoration of oversight, the codification of criteria, and the establishment of many new regulatory burdens focused on information provision by the agencies. While the agencies complain about these burdens, the business models of the agencies remain unchanged, and how they come to their judgments remains their own business, with no substantial interference from outside parties, including government agencies in the United States and Europe. While rating agencies are certainly chastened by the crisis—they experienced extensive criticism and were challenged repeatedly to account for their dealings, as I show in chapter 5—they are still there, they still make lots of money, and while what they do is watched more closely now, they still have the independence they had before the crisis, and their role has not been seriously reduced.

Bad, Bad, Bad

Like the rating agencies, the financial crisis that started in 2007 remains an enigma. By now, most people think they know what that crisis was all about and how it was caused. The popular account focuses on bad behavior by bad people in bad institutions.[2] Because of greed, and because people did not do their jobs properly, money was lent to people who could not possibly pay it back. Part of the blame for the crisis is attributed to those seeking to finance a home. Lending to subprime borrowers—those whose credit history or circumstances (such as lack of employment) meant they could not borrow at normal or prime rates—was a mistake, and as soon as these mortgages started to fail the financial system came unstuck.

Banks (of all types) were bad too. Banks and other mortgage originators should not have lent to these borrowers, and government should not have condoned this process via implicit support for Fannie Mae and Freddie Mac, the US government–sponsored housing enterprises. The financial innovation built on subprime by investment banks was excessive and would inevitably bring disaster, according to this now commonsense view. As soon as people realized housing prices would not keep rising indefinitely in the United States, this house of cards started to collapse. Assets became toxic or unsaleable. Institutions whose balance sheets were suddenly dominated by these toxic assets had to be supported by the taxpayer to avoid collapse. These government bailouts stimulated deep public unhappiness with politics and the banking system.

According to this account, the rating agencies were key players in the germination of the financial crisis. The job of the agencies is

---

2. See, for example, Dean Baker, *Plunder and Blunder: The Rise and Fall of the Bubble Economy* (Sausalito, CA: PoliPointPress, 2009); and Lawrence G. McDonald with Patrick Robinson, *A Colossal Failure of Common Sense: The Inside Story of the Collapse of Lehman Brothers* (New York: Crown, 2009). For a more recent scholarly account, which addresses the question of whether there was choice for government agencies in Lehman's demise, see Laurence M. Ball, *The Fed and Lehman Brothers: Setting the Record Straight on a Financial Disaster* (New York: Cambridge University Press, 2018).

to provide impartial information and make judgments about the likely repayment of securities in the future. The agencies have made many mistakes about this in the past. Perhaps their most spectacular error was the rating of Enron Corporation, which filed for bankruptcy on December 2, 2001. In this case, the agencies missed the intricate financial engineering that supported Enron. The agencies were also guilty of being slow to adapt and of being not nearly as smart as they should have been about financial innovation. In the established view, the agencies were, like the mortgage originators, the investment banks, and subprime borrowers, greedy, irresponsible, and inept.[3]

Because the agencies obtained their income from the fees paid by issuers of bonds for the rating of their debt, the agencies had strong incentives to rate anything presented to them positively, according to this line of thinking. This relationship suggested to many that the agencies have a conflict of interest because they are paid to rate bonds by the issuers of those bonds, who normally want the highest ratings they can get.[4]

The widely held view suggests that the agencies provided inflated ratings for the bonds associated with subprime lending. Given that many subprime borrowers had low or unstable incomes, or a his-

---

3. Robert Shiller has explored how accounts like this one develop and become the dominant understanding of events. Robert J. Shiller, *Narrative Economics: How Stories Go Viral and Drive Major Economic Events* (Princeton, NJ: Princeton University Press, 2019). Also see Mitchel Y. Abolafia, "Narrative Construction as Sensemaking: How a Central Bank Thinks," *Organization Studies* 31, no. 3 (2010): 349–367; and Mitchel Y. Abolafia, *Stewards of the Market: How the Federal Reserve Made Sense of the Financial Crisis* (Cambridge, MA: Harvard University Press, 2020).

4. This is a popular view but does not explain why the conflict of interest suddenly became a problem in 2008, even though the agencies started charging issuers fees for ratings from the late 1960s onward. On this puzzle, see Ann Rutledge and Robert E. Litan, "A Real Fix for Credit Ratings," *Economic Studies at Brookings*, Brookings Institution, Washington, DC, June 2014, i.

tory of financial problems, for many observers it makes no sense that some of the bonds associated with subprime lending were rated AAA. Giving these bonds such strong ratings must somehow reflect deep corruption in the rating business.[5]

The rating agencies were no longer providing unbiased opinions, the conventional wisdom suggests. They were going after maximum income just like everybody else associated with the real estate market at the time. Once people realized these ratings were inflated there was a crisis on Wall Street as counterparties—financial institutions engaged in trading financial securities with each other—no longer had confidence the financial instruments they had invested in were sound.

More recently, grafted onto the drama and emotion of these accounts have been insights into some of the key mechanisms of the crisis provided by acute observers such as Michael Lewis.[6] The effect of this work has been to create a wider appreciation of the degree to which the opaqueness and connectedness of complex financial instruments were at the core of the Wall Street crisis.

A Different View

As a step toward understanding the role of the rating agencies, this book offers a different view of what gave rise to the financial crisis that began in 2007.[7] The key difference between the account

---

5. Barry Ritholtz has described the Big Three as engaged in a form of payola. Payola was the practice of radio stations playing records for payments, boosting record sales and chart positions. See Ritholtz with Aaron Task, *Bailout Nation: How Greed and Easy Money Corrupted Wall Street and Shook the World Economy* (New York: John Wiley, 2009), 111.

6. Michael Lewis, *The Big Short: Inside the Doomsday Machine* (New York: Norton, 2010). This book was made into a film in 2015.

7. Other scholars have suggested that the standard view of the crisis makes too much of financial market events altogether. What is of greater significance

of the crisis offered here, and the usual story, is that in my understanding crisis is a normal, if not daily, event in financial markets. Crisis should not be understood as aberrant and exogenous, but as endogenous, as being caused by the markets themselves. The problem with most conventional understandings of the global financial crisis is that they make markets into utopias that are self-regulating and not subject to failure. As a result, these accounts cannot acknowledge the endogenous nature of market crises. In the conventional account, crises only occur because people do bad or illegal things, or because there is some defect or "failure" in institutions, perhaps caused by government. Crises are therefore exogenous to markets, reflecting problems external to them. Markets cannot be blamed for crises.

Although people do bad things, institutions fail, and governments mess things up, this is not at the core of what happened to bring about the global financial crisis. A key feature of the financial markets is a perpetual search for yield on assets. When interest rates are low, as they were in the years following the dot-com bust of 2000/2001, financial markets tend to look for better returns in new places and new ways. At various points in the past this led to a flow of funds from the rich countries to emerging markets where higher returns were available. But the political uncertainties associated with these flows were always problematic because the willingness to repay was open to doubt.

Rather than the search for yield leading to an external flow, this time around resources went into financial innovation in the United States. That innovation was associated with risk management in the

---

for Scott Sumner is what he sees as the failed policy responses that magnify the problems on Wall Street into a national and subsequently global crisis. See Scott B. Sumner, "Ten Lessons from the Economic Crisis of 2008," *Cato Journal* 39, no. 2 (2019): 449–459.

mortgage finance business. This risk management consisted of removing the risk of default on these mortgages from the books of mortgage lenders through a process called securitization. This process, which involved making the financial flows from illiquid assets like car loans, credit card receivables, and home mortgages into liquid, tradeable bonds, strengthened the balance sheets of the mortgage lenders or originators, allowing them to lend even more to house buyers, and created a new pool of financial assets, such as collateralized debt obligations (CDOs), which could be traded between financial institutions, providing opportunities for arbitrage, or buying in one market and selling in another, by investment banks.[8] In a context of low interest rates and the hunt for yield, structured finance grew to around $10.7 trillion in value at its height. This was less than 10 percent of the total value of global financial market instruments, which was $138.4 trillion at the end of 2006. Just $0.7 trillion of this total were subprime residential mortgage-backed securities (RMBS).[9]Although the amount of money associated with subprime lending was relatively low, RMBS, especially CDOs built on top of subprime lending, were a lucrative form of financial innovation and attractive to many participants in the financial markets. These offered higher returns with stronger credit ratings.

Euphoria started to attach itself to these assets as financial market participants saw the returns available. Like similar eruptions of financial market euphoria in the past, the most comparable being the 1920s real estate boom in Florida, new information that tended to cast doubt on the quality of these assets led markets to respond

---

8. On securitization, see Sylvain Raynes and Ann Rutledge, *The Analysis of Structured Securities: Precise Risk Measurement and Capital Allocation* (New York: Oxford University Press, 2003); and Ann Rutledge and Sylvain Raynes, *Elements of Structured Finance* (New York: Oxford University Press, 2010).

9. Bank of England, *Financial Stability Report*, London, October 2007, 20.

periodically with fright. So, when some mildly negative information about subprime defaults emerged in spring 2007, the market reaction was much more negative than would otherwise be expected.

Subsequently, a series of reports, including announcements by the credit rating agencies about revisions to their methodology, began a process, gradually at first, then picking up steam, in which euphoria turned into panic. Bear Stearns was sold at a great discount to JP Morgan in early 2008 after the failure of two of its subprime mortgage funds. The Lehman Brothers bankruptcy in September 2008 and the subsequent American International Group (AIG) bailout are moments of this gathering panic, in which financial assets suddenly were transformed into what came to be known as toxic assets.

While the rating agencies may well employ people who do bad things, just like any other organization, what is missing from the conventional account is any substantial evidence of malfeasance on the part of the rating agencies. What seems to have occurred is more mundane but actually more worrying.

Contribution of the Agencies

At least three things are key to the direct contribution of the rating agencies to the germination of the crisis. First, there is the problem of how to incorporate future events into ratings. Ratings cannot just assume imminent Armageddon. Issuing ratings anticipates some sort of normal, reasonable future. If ratings always assumed Armageddon, other things being equal, very few ratings, if any, would be anything other than speculative grade. But, of course, what transpired in 2008 and 2009 was—in the absence of concerted action by the US government—very much like the start of Armageddon. Like everyone else prior to the onset of crisis, the agencies assumed a large measure of continuity. They factored in business cycle downturns, as they have done with rating corporate bonds for decades. What they did not do is anticipate a deep, geographically widespread market crisis. Assuming things will be largely similar in the future, and so underestimating change, proved to be a mistake. This is the sort of error many businesses and governments make. It is hard to predict the future and even harder to predict the specific characteristics of the future.

The second contribution made by the agencies to the development of the crisis is the curious fact that the rating agencies were not rating the quality of the original financial assets, the mortgages that underpinned RMBS. Although most people assume that this is what they were doing, the agencies were rating something else. The agencies were rating claims on the flows of funds that emerged from these mortgages. The logic of this is that claims could be legally distinguished one from another using trusts, which are characterized by claims to assets organized in tranches. Some tranches of bonds would have stronger legal claims than others to the flow of funds (and so would receive cash first from people paying their mortgages). This was the basis for awarding the strongest claims a AAA rating. The idea was they would never fail to pay, even if lower-rated tranches defaulted. This model of credit protection turned out to be unreliable as conditions worsened, and so proved a mistake.

The third contribution is that the agencies strayed from their traditional role. Most of this book focuses on this shift. Moody's was floated as a new public company in 2000. This development may have changed the identity of the company. The conventional explanation suggests that the agencies were simply going after the money, and so rating everything strongly to earn high fees. A variant of the greed argument uses the language of conflict of interest. It focuses on the fact that the agencies are paid by the issuers of debt, as mentioned earlier. The argument is that this incentivizes the agencies to inflate ratings to keep those who pay for ratings happy. This is a popular argument, although, as I noted, it does not explain why conflict of interest is suddenly a problem in 2007 despite existing since the late 1960s.

I suggest that *the agencies stopped working as judges of the process and started working as advisers to the process.* The key role of the agencies during the twentieth century had been to offer disinterested advice, to play the role of referee or judge in the debt markets. This role is like that of auditors. Now, the agencies started to provide advice to issuers on how to organize financial contracts to meet the thresholds for the different tranches and their respective flows of funds. By advising on the construction of financial instruments like this the agencies threatened their standing as disinterested judges of the financial instruments of others. The lack of critical distance fed back into the failure to anticipate the crisis, weak scrutiny of the originating credit quality, and the development of market skepticism about their judgments. Not sticking closely to their core role was a catastrophic mistake by the agencies.

Three Puzzles

I explore three puzzles in this book. The first puzzle is why the agencies put their franchise at such risk prior to the crisis. Bad choices by institutions are quite normal, the substance of everyday life, and are therefore not puzzling in themselves. What is puzzling is when institutions make choices that seem, at least to the outside observer, to undermine their very reason for being. The rating agencies did this when they decided to advise their clients on the design of structured financial products that would achieve certain rating outcomes. This active role robbed the agencies of their established image as putatively disinterested parties, exposing them to accusations of partiality. This mostly took the public form of criticism of the conflict of interest inherent in the agencies taking payment from issuers for rating their bond issues. Why did the agencies take such massive risks with their franchise? Why did they not see this activity as potentially self-destructive? What was it that pushed these institutions, which had been steadfastly conservative for decades, to change their behavior so dramatically?

The second puzzle is—given the scale and gravity of the crisis, and the many parties willing to blame the agencies for creating or aggravating the crisis—how it is that the agencies managed to survive? Despite undermining their franchise by advising issuers on how to structure their issues to achieve specific ratings, they managed to avoid the fate that befell Arthur Andersen when it surrendered its CPA license in 2002 following the collapse of Enron Corporation. Indeed, the agencies have thrived since the crisis and demonstrated their renewed relevance during the European sovereign debt crisis that began in 2010. Why have the agencies survived seemingly unscathed, and not been displaced or replaced by alternatives? What are the prospects for the development of rating agencies in ways that make them return to a disinterested, countercyclical role that offers assurance to investors and public goods to society in terms of dampening market volatility?

The final puzzle is why what I term the exogenous approach to understanding financial crises has continued to dominate the interpretation of the global financial crisis and the role of the agencies in the crisis, despite "a new heterogeneity of thinking" Jonathan Kirshner identifies outside the United States.[10] Given the scale and

---

10. Jonathan Kirshner, *American Power after the Financial Crisis* (Ithaca, NY: Cornell University Press, 2014), 2.

gravity of the crisis you might think an approach that offered a more systemic account of the crisis, one that considered what it is about finance itself that produces crises, would have become the mainstream or hegemonic interpretation, as occurred in the wake of the Great Depression. But a critical view of finance did not develop following the crisis that began in 2007. Instead of blaming banking, bankers were blamed. Someone was found to blame instead of the mechanisms, institutions, and social relations that lie at the center of finance. As we know from movies about the old West, once the bad guy has been dealt with the crime is forgotten. The exogenous approach to crisis remains the dominant view, and it continues to shape the collective understanding of the role of the agencies in the crisis. This book examines the assuagement process as it relates to credit rating.

Two Arguments

Why did the agencies risk their franchise by switching to an advisory role, telling clients what they needed, and helping issuers obtain the ratings they required to create their structured finance products? What we need to get to grips with is what dislocated a long-entrenched conservative rating mentality, a system and set of habits that had been established in these Wall Street institutions for decades. The broadest context for what happened is the disintermediation of finance, in which borrowers seek funds in the capital markets directly, rather than borrowing from banks.[11] Disinterme-

---

11. Lena Rethel and Timothy J. Sinclair, *The Problem with Banks* (London: Zed Books, 2012). For a more recent, thoughtful discussion of these and related issues, see Adair Turner, *Between Debt and the Devil: Money, Credit, and Fixing Global Finance* (Princeton, NJ: Princeton University Press, 2016), especially chap. 10.

diation mobilized banks to pursue securitized finance. RMBS offered higher returns but with the alluring prospect of strong credit ratings.

Why did the agencies embrace their changed role in securitized finance, even at the risk of destroying their rating franchise? My argument is that after the Enron disaster the agencies were uncertain about the rating business. They did not know what disasters lay around the next corner for them, given financial innovation.[12] Their old model of how to operate no longer seemed relevant in these circumstances. Moody's canvassed market opinion about themselves and their output around this time. They might have stuck to their guns or even become more conservative. But they did not. They changed a great deal in ways that made them almost unrecognizable.

Compounding this acute uncertainty was the rise of Fitch. Fitch changed a comfortable duopoly into a three-way oligopoly, making the agencies acutely sensitive to the shrinkage of their market share. Under the duopoly, Moody's and S&P were guaranteed to rate an issue, given the norm of two ratings per security. But that same norm meant that one of the now three major agencies would miss out on the business once Fitch became a viable choice for issuers. If Fitch had not managed to become a member of what became the Big Three, the agencies may well have taken a more arm's-length relationship to structured finance, and it may never have become the business it became.

My second argument concerns the survival of the agencies. While the agencies failed, they did not die, as did Enron and Enron's audit firm, Arthur Andersen. Moody's, S&P, and Fitch remain highly

---

12. This was a feature of my discussions with a senior Moody's official in March 2002, in the wake of Enron and the collapse of the World Trade Center twin towers, which were adjacent to Moody's New York headquarters.

profitable. There may be elements of atonement or redemption about the survival of the agencies, but it is the continued functioning of the agencies that is most interesting, despite the odds stacked against them. How did these institutions that have been accused of terrible wrongdoing, incompetence, and corruption go on, and what marks out this persistence from the institutions that did not survive? The central question about the survival of the agencies is whether their continued existence is a matter of good fortune, because they happen to be in a strategic position and thus necessary, or whether their survival has been orchestrated by the agencies themselves. Other things being equal, if survival is merely functional, and thus the good luck of the agencies to be essential in specific circumstances, with the passage of time, the rise of new institutions and new circumstances should bring change. If the rating agencies are not perceived to be doing a good job, people will look for alternatives even if they must put up with the rating system for now. In these circumstances, like bookstores and many other institutions that have faded away in recent years as their business models have evaporated, the agencies may find themselves without a role. If the agencies' hand in their own survival is more active, they may have a brighter future.

I think there is a two-pronged explanation for the persistence of the agencies. The first aspect concerns homeostasis. We do not have institutions that do what they do better than the rating agencies, despite whatever failings we attribute to them. The other dimension to survival of the agencies is the continuing dominance of the Big Three. The top agencies, Moody's, S&P, and Fitch, have not given way to the many smaller, less prominent agencies in the years since the crisis began, despite blame being directed toward the Big Three and efforts to open the rating market by authorities in the United States and Europe. I argue that the continued dominance of the Big Three reflects the necessity in ratings that some judgments have more weight than others. This bias to a small set of rating agencies is essential if ratings are to have any significance or authority to investors. Concentration of market share in a few hands reflects what ratings provide to those who use them. Reputation is exclusive and favors incumbents.[13]

A Supporting Argument

My final argument is harder to conclusively substantiate, so I give it a supporting status in this book. This claim, about the continuing vitality of the exogenous view of crises, is that comment by politicians, regulators, experts, the financial press, and the wider media identifying a bad guy, a villain, as we see with the rating agencies and financial crisis, is best understood as part of a process of assuagement in a complex, massive failure like the global financial crisis. Focusing on the bad guy offers a way of relieving public and professional anger. In making this argument I am not suggesting that the agencies are blameless. I suggest that broad processes such as financial innovation are hard for most people to think about concretely, and may point to financial markets themselves as problematic. The search for bad guys and for developing limited "Band-Aid" solutions may, I suggest, be about reducing the damage failure causes to the collective belief in the coherence and legitimacy of the broader system. A strategy of assuagement that focuses on institutions that appear to be outside finance has the advantage of being concrete and specific, and focused on the failure

---

13. Giulia Mennillo and Timothy J. Sinclair, "A Hard Nut to Crack: Regulatory Failure Shows How Rating Really Works," *Competition and Change* 23, no. 3 (2019): 270.

of things other than the financial markets themselves. Rating agencies are not financial institutions. They are professional services firms, like lawyers and accountants, that make finance possible. Seeing rating agencies as external or exogenous reinforces the idea that finance itself is not the problem, only the human institutions that interact with finance, like the agencies.

Approach

Thirty years ago, the scholarly writing about the agencies was dominated by business school financial economists. This work typically sought to identify what was central to rating determination and what was not, to help the issuers of bonds secure a better rating and thus lower funding costs. What was common to this work and its contemporary equivalent is the idea that rating is, or should be, a technical matter.[14] Underlying this expectation was the assumption that there are correct and incorrect ways to do rating, just as there are correct and incorrect ways to install spark plugs or swim backstroke.

It would be good if things were as simple as this. But it turns out that trying to understand rating this way is of limited veracity. Un-

---

14. A typical example of this sort of work is Herwig Langohr and Patricia Langohr, *The Rating Agencies and Their Credit Ratings: What They Are, How They Work, and Why They Are Relevant* (Chichester, UK: Wiley, 2008). Other works in this vein include Onjewu Adah-Kole Emmanuel, *The Role of Credit Rating Agencies in the Financial Crisis: Definitive Conclusion from Grounded Theory* (Saarbrücken, Germany: Lambert, 2011); Gianluca Mattarocci, *The Independence of Credit Rating Agencies: How Business Models and Regulators Interact* (Oxford: Elsevier, 2014); Raquel García Alcubilla and Javier Ruiz Del Pozo, *Credit Rating Agencies on the Watch List: Analysis of European Regulation* (Oxford: Oxford University Press, 2012); John De Luca and Paul Russo, eds., *Credit Rating Agency Reform* (New York: Nova Science, 2009). An interesting contribution, based on experience in the rating agencies, is Roger P. Nye, *Understanding and Managing the Credit Rating Agencies* (London: Euromoney Institutional Investor, 2014).

surprisingly, as a consequence, authorities have made little progress in addressing the rating enigma. The approach taken by most people to rating is synchronic. This mentality, which is about solving problems, focuses on the properties of the system. Such an approach makes sense when the properties are fixed, such as they are in, say, an automobile engine. The synchronic approach is a sensible one for many practical problems. For designing apartment buildings and food mixers, thinking about the properties of a system as fixed makes sense most of the time.

A different approach is required for thinking about institutions in the social world, because social life is much more dynamic than nature.[15] The diachronic approach suggests that understanding the properties of a system, like a specific institution, is just the first step to obtaining the full picture. We also need to understand the potential for change inherent in the institution. This suggests a longer-term, organic approach that appreciates that change may go in different directions, given different circumstances. The future is not fixed by the properties of the system, although these characteristics may make some outcomes more likely than others.

In addition to adopting this more historical and evolutionary way of thinking about the agencies, we also need to adopt what I call a social foundations approach. The essence of this way of thinking can be found in John Maynard Keynes's "beauty contest metaphor." Keynes argued that people in the financial markets do not

---

15. I am indebted to Robert W. Cox's development of these ideas, as collected in Robert W. Cox with Timothy J. Sinclair, *Approaches to World Order* (Cambridge: Cambridge University Press, 1996). For an analysis of how I have developed the approach and used it in my research, see Rudra Sil and Peter J. Katzenstein, *Beyond Paradigms: Analytic Eclecticism in the Study of World Politics* (London: Palgrave Macmillan, 2010). The book examines my approach on pages 118–125. My own statement about my work appears in box 4.2 on page 124.

think about the fundamental merits of an investment in isolation. They are, instead, focused on outdoing their rivals in the markets. He illustrated this by invoking the English tabloid newspaper beauty competitions of the 1930s.[16] Readers could win these competitions not by picking the prettiest face but by guessing which face most other readers would think most attractive. So, the competition was not about a fundamental or absolute form of knowledge but about estimating collective thinking correctly. Since Keynes's time the calculative techniques deployed to make money via financial speculation have developed greatly. Confidence in these tools of calculation among market participants "as ostensibly scientific, legitimate and [as] more than mere speculation" is an important dimension of the social foundations approach.[17]

Collective thinking, including calculative techniques, is fundamental to the rating product, as the authority or brand of a rating agency is central to the success of its business. The agencies have no tangible product, unlike a steelmaker or even a bank. All they have is an intangible reputation for good judgment. While in certain circumstances ratings are mandated by the US government and other governments around the world, Moody's, S&P, and Fitch have most of the rating market because other agencies do not have the hold on collective thinking these three global agencies enjoy. Some rating agencies are internationally important. Most are not. I will largely ignore the—for the present—globally unimportant agencies in this book, and new rating activities, such as environmental, social, and governance ratings.[18]

---

16. John Maynard Keynes, *The General Theory of Employment, Interest, and Money* (Amherst, NY: Prometheus, 1997 [1936]), chap. 12, p. 156.

17. E-mail from Paul Langley to the author, January 8, 2019.

18. An example is China's Dagong. See "China's Dagong Global Credit Mounts Challenge to 'Big Three' Rating Agencies," *South China Morning Post,* August 7,

Plan of the Book

In chapter 2, I examine what it is the agencies do. Here I explain what ratings are, how the rating process works, and the process of financial disintermediation that has changed the context for the agencies so dramatically. I examine the rating market as it is today and discuss the regulation of the agencies, including the implications of the Dodd-Frank Act passed in 2010 and the policy work of the Financial Stability Board.

In the following chapter I examine different ways of thinking about the agencies and argue that the social foundations approach is the most effective approach. Rather than focus on the full range of thinking about the agencies, I have focused on the main strands, beginning with market-centered approaches. After considering populist views of the agencies and the critical perspective, I make a case for the social foundations approach.

Chapter 4 dives into structured finance and the agencies' involvement in rating this form of financial innovation. I explain how securitization worked, what the agencies did in the process, and the implications of their work for the structured finance market. The chapter then considers the second thoughts the agencies had about these products and the effect of this development on the markets. The chapter concludes with a discussion of the repurchase markets and how the shift in sentiment rebounded through this vast financial space.

2016, http://www.scmp.com/business/banking-finance/article/2000489/chinas
-dagong-global-credit-mounts-challenge-big-three, accessed August 16, 2016. For
insight on these agencies, see Ginevra Marandola, "Local Credit Rating Agencies: A
New Dataset," *Research in International Business and Finance* 38 (September 2016):
83–103. On environmental, social, and governance ratings, see Billy Nauman,
"Credit Rating Agencies Join Battle for ESG Supremacy," *Moral Money MSCI* Inc
(part of the *Financial Times*), September 17, 2019, https://www.ft.com/content
/59f60306-d671-11e9-8367-807ebd53ab77, accessed September 22, 2019.

In chapter 5 I interrogate the first argument of this book about the impact of financial innovation and increased competition in the rating market, largely through an examination of US congressional hearings and hearings by British members of Parliament that scrutinized the crisis and the role of the agencies in these events. The postcrisis survival of the agencies is the focus of chapter 6. This chapter, also based in great part on hearing testimony, argues that homeostasis or systemic conservatism was significant, and that the dominance of the Big Three has become a constitutive feature of the market for ratings. In making this case the chapter examines rating and the European sovereign debt crisis, the rating downgrade of the United States, competition, and transparency issues.

The final substantive chapter of the book is an addendum in which I make a case for my supplementary argument about assuagement. This chapter examines exogenous and endogenous explanations for financial crises and suggests that the agencies are labeled as exogenous institutions, strengthening the argument that the mistakes they make cannot be attributed to finance itself, reducing the pressure for change in the purpose and governance of financial markets. I have styled this chapter as an addendum to signal that these arguments are necessarily more speculative than the first two.

Chapter 8 concludes this book by considering questions of blame, the possibility of a role for government in rating, the merits of a social foundations view of the agencies, the role of financial innovation in creating disaster, whether rating has changed, what we want from rating (and what we should want), the scope for future rating research, and the ongoing rating enigma.

2

The Agencies and What They Do

Bond-rating agency Moody's Investors Service used to
be an ivory tower of finance. Analysts were discouraged from having a drink with a client. Phone calls
from bankers went unanswered if they rang during
intense, almost academic debates about credit ratings.
—*Aaron Lucchetti*, Wall Street Journal

Rating agencies are a familiar part of the financial system. People
think they know what the agencies do and how they operate.
But there are many misconceptions about them. Some people seem
to think the agencies were created by government. The lack of understanding of the agencies is shared by people in the markets, politicians, government officials, and commentators. Many people
seem to mistakenly think the agencies produce information that has
the same standing as an audit report. In addition to not really know-
ing what the agencies do, there is a tendency to exaggerate the importance of rating, or sometimes to assume rating is the only form
of financial analysis necessary to good decision making about investment. Given all these misconceptions, it is important to get an
understanding of what rating agencies do and what they do not do,
and what may be the implications of their work before we examine the major arguments of this book in later chapters.

While rating may have been a dull, quiet, behind-the-scenes activity many years ago, the process of disintermediation has made the agencies and what they do more important over time in the United States, in Europe, and in Asia. The emergence of the agencies into a central role in the global financial system only really came to light when there were problems with rating companies like Enron and the RMBS products at the center of the global financial crisis.

This chapter examines some basic facts and concepts associated with the rating agencies. I start off by asking what ratings are and then examine the rating process. In the section that follows I look at financial disintermediation, the broad trend that is making rating agencies more important than they were in the past. This is followed by a discussion of the contemporary rating market and then an examination of the regulation of the rating agencies.

What Are Ratings?

Ratings may seem obscure and mundane. They are, in fact, an enormously ambitious form of human knowledge. The ambition stems from their purpose, which is to forecast what is going to happen in the future to large sums of money. This is a very challenging thing to do, and necessarily involves a considerable measure of judgment. As rating failures, culminating in the global financial crisis, have demonstrated, you cannot simply derive ratings from an observation of the facts. Producing ratings involves making assumptions about what could happen in the future in which the raters think some scenarios more likely than others. Rather than being measurements, as people may assume, ratings are better understood as ideas about, or theorizations of, the future. Within that theorization—like all theorizations—there is great scope for confusion, hidden agendas, and shoddy workmanship.

Part of the mindset that assumes ratings are—or should be—measurements of creditworthiness is the conflation of ability and willingness to repay.[1] Ability to repay is the capacity within the financial resources available to the issuer to make interest and principal repayments on schedule. The willingness to repay is an assessment of the determination of the issuer to repay even if circumstances change or if management changes. The question of willingness is why credit rating agencies are interested in corporate management, business plans, governance, and the prospects for policymaking in the case of public entities affected by political processes. Ratings are not just a measure of the financial health of the issuer, but whether that issuer is focused on repayment, or perhaps has other priorities or problems that might interfere with repayment.

The rating agencies emphasize the limited purpose of ratings. Moody's, for example, say that ratings "should not be used as a basis for investment operations."[2] Although ratings are "judgements about the future," they do not offer guidance on future trends in market price.[3] Market price, they note, reflects credit quality but also market circumstances and broader economic conditions. Despite not offering guidance on where market price will go in the future, Moody's look at negative future scenarios for repayment, because they say they understand that investors want to use ratings as "a means of protection."[4] Moody's note that ratings are "statements of opinion and not statements of fact," and that they are not

---

1. On the increasing significance of creditworthiness, see Michel Feher, *Rated Agency: Investee Politics in a Speculative Age* (New York: Zone Books, 2018).
2. See Moody's Investors Service, "Limitations to Uses of Ratings," https://www.moodys.com/ratings-process/Ratings-Definitions/002002, accessed August 15, 2016.
3. Moody's, "Limitations."
4. Moody's, "Limitations."

TABLE 1
Credit Rating Scales

Moody's	Fitch/S&P
Aaa	AAA
Aa	AA
A	A
Baa	BBB
Ba	BB
B	B
Caa	CCC
Ca	CC
C	C
N/A	RD*/D/NR

*Fitch uses the category Restricted Default or RD to refer to the circumstance in which nonpayment is selective or partial. NR is an S&P designation that indicates no rating has been requested, that S&P does not have enough information to issue a rating, or that S&P does not rate an obligation type as a matter of policy. See S&P, "Long-Term Issue Credit Ratings," https://www.standardandpoors.com/en_US/web/guest/article/-/view/sourceId/504352, accessed August 15, 2016.

recommendations to investors to buy or sell securities. Importantly, investors must do their homework, state Moody's: "Each rating or other opinion must be weighed solely as one factor in any investment decision made by or on behalf of any user of the information, and each such user must accordingly make its own study and evaluation of each security and of each issuer."[5] The ratings and their arrangement in scales or tables matured in the 1920s. The classic formulation is for bonds or long-term debt with maturities of six months or more, as depicted in table 1. Moody's refers to these symbols as their "Global Long-Term Rating Scale."

---

5. Moody's, "Limitations."

What does the market make of the agencies? Prior to the Enron crash in 2001 there had been frequent but muted criticism of the agencies for decades. The main theme of this commentary in the financial press was that the agencies were thought to be too historically focused, too backward-looking, and that they did not react fast enough to changing circumstances by warning investors as issuers ran into trouble that might threaten their ability to repay. Commentators then—as now—were disappointed the agencies did not anticipate all the complexities of financial innovation and were, like army generals, applying the lessons of past problems to current issues when new thinking was needed.

Since the global financial crisis began this criticism has become much more vocal and wide-ranging.[6] Condemnation, vitriol, and abuse were characteristic of much of the commentary about the agencies in the years 2007–2009. One author compared the agencies to the creators of horoscopes.[7] More recently, when a rating downgrade is threatened the reaction may be nonchalant.[8] The fact

6. Constantine von Hoffman, "Why Are the Ratings Agencies Still in Business?," *CBS News*, May 3, 2012, http://www.cbsnews.com/news/why-are-the-ratings-agencies-still-in-business/, accessed May 3, 2012.

7. Girish Menon, "Ratings Agencies—The Power of Modern Day Astrologers," *Global Policy*, June 29, 2012, http://www.globalpolicyjournal.com/blog/29/06/2012/ratings-agencies-power-modern-day-astrologers, accessed August 15, 2016.

8. Stephen Grenville, "Australia's AAA Credit Rating under Threat, but Who Cares?," *The Interpreter*, July 11, 2016, http://www.lowyinterpreter.org/post/2016/07/11/Australias-AAA-credit-rating-under-threat-but-who-cares.aspx, accessed August 15, 2016; Ross Gittins, "Oh No, Not a Credit Rating Downgrade," *Sydney Morning Herald*, July 10, 2016, https://www.smh.com.au/business/ross-gittins-oh-no-not-a-credit-rating-downgrade-20160709-gq25vg.html, accessed July 10, 2016; Martin O'Rourke, "Do Credit Rating Agencies Still Matter?," TradingFloor.com, April 9, 2016, https://www.tradingfloor.com/posts/do-credit-rating-agencies-still-matter-7418030, accessed June 14, 2018. On sovereign ratings, see Matthew Lynn, "Opinion: About to Lose Your Triple-A Credit Rating? No One Cares Anymore," *MarketWatch*, November 11, 2015, https://www.marketwatch.com/story

that the agencies' business model is reliant on payment of fees by the issuers of securities that the agencies rate suggests to many observers that there is a conflict of interest at the heart of the rating process, and that the agencies are corrupt.[9]

For the most part, the business of rating securities has continued uninterrupted and unhindered by these hostile views. The idea that ratings matter, that they are highly consequential and a core feature of the markets, has not, despite the negative views held by many market participants, budged much, if at all, since 2007.[10]

/about-to-lose-your-triple-a-credit-rating-no-one-cares-anymore-2015-11-11, accessed November 11, 2015. For a systematic treatment, see Dimitrios Soudis, "Credit Rating Agencies and the IPE: Not as Influential as Thought?," *Review of International Political Economy* 22, no. 4 (2015): 813–837. Also see Dimitrios Soudis, *Looking under the Hood: Embedded Actors and Local Institutions in the Making of Globalization* (Groningen, the Netherlands: University of Groningen, 2014).

9. On the conflict of interest issue, see Charles W. Calomiris and Stephen H. Haber, *Fragile by Design: The Political Origins of Banking Crises and Scarce Credit* (Princeton, NJ: Princeton University Press, 2014), 266–269. Also see John Kay, *The Long and the Short of It* (London: Erasmus Press, 2009), 164.

10. Mahir Binici, Michael Hutchison, and Evan Weicheng Miao, "Are Credit Rating Agencies Discredited? Measuring Market Price Effects from Agency Sovereign Debt Announcements," Bank for International Settlements, BIS Working Papers, No. 704, February 2018; Patrick Kingsley, "How Credit Ratings Agencies Rule the World," *The Guardian*, February 12, 2012, https://www.theguardian.com /business/2012/feb/15/credit-ratings-agencies-moodys, accessed February 18, 2016; Rick Salutin, "Bond Rating Agencies Have a Lot of Nerve: Salutin," *Toronto Star*, July 17, 2014, https://www.thestar.com/opinion/commentary/2014/07/17 /bond_rating_agencies_have_a_lot_of_nerve_salutin.html, accessed July 21, 2014. Also see Nouriel Roubini, "Rating Agencies Still Matter—and That Is Inexcusable," *Financial Times*, August 10, 2015, https://www.ft.com/content/750fc7b0-3f41 -11e5-b98b-87c7270955cf, accessed August 10, 2015; Kai Ryssdal, "Big Three Credit Rating Agencies Still Hold a Huge Amount of Power," *Marketplace*, March 11, 2016, https://www.marketplace.org/2016/03/11/world/big-three-credit -ratings-agencies-still-hold-huge-amount-power, accessed March 11, 2016. For an exhaustive review of the issue, see Fernando Gonzalez et al., "Market Dynamics

Moody's, S&P, and Fitch have 95 percent of the global rating market, "a total virtually unchanged from before the financial crisis."[11] Moody's Corporation, the parent of Moody's Investors Service, did see significant change in the corporation's stock price during the crisis. The stock fell to just $18 from $80 in 2009. But the same stock was trading on the New York Stock Exchange at $226.53 on December 2, 2019, at 9.34 a.m., close to the stock's all-time high.[12] Moody's net profit margin at the time was 30.58 percent, a couple of points lower than JPMorgan Chase & Co. (32.63 percent), but better than Apple at 21.37 percent, almost twice that of Alphabet Inc. (owner of Google) at 17.45 percent, and more than six times that of Exxon Mobil (5 percent).

Like most professionals that do highly consequential work, raters tend to take the significance of credit rating agencies for granted. For many younger staffers it is their entry into employment in the financial industry, before moving on to a bank or other institution. Interviews with very senior people in the agencies over the years gave me the impression they conceive of ratings as a feature of a "system" and that they expect market participants to involve themselves in the requirements of that system. Given the idea of

---

Associated with Credit Ratings: A Literature Review," European Central Bank, Occasional Paper Series, No. 16, June 2004.

11. Timothy W. Martin, "Moody's Profit Falls, Hurt by Foreign Exchange," *Wall Street Journal*, February 5, 2016, http://www.wsj.com/articles/moodys-profit -falls-hurt-by-foreign-exchange-1454676926, accessed August 19, 2016.

12. Data taken from NYSE: https://www.google.com/search?rlz=1C1CHBF _en-GBGB831GB831&tbm=fin&sxsrf=ACYBGNT3Ac19JW-PRqpwyXQ6O4m dcy4sDw:1575296276124&q=NYSE:+MCO&stick=H4sIAAAAAAAAAONgecR oyi3w8sc9YSmdSWtOXmNU4-IKzsgvd80rySypFJLgYoOy-KR4uLj0c _UNzKuyK8oMeBaxcvpFBrtaKfg6-wMAXMZQO0YAAAA&biw=1536&bih =722#scso=_-yDlXb_lG5TXgQbMy6qoAg5:0.

ratings as part of a system, the idea of unsolicited ratings, where the agencies rate corporations and governments without request, makes sense, as the rating agencies need to be sure their system is complete.

A wise and eloquent senior rating official, now long retired, suggested to me that rating agency workers could be divided into two groups. The first group did what they did like most employees, with professionalism but perhaps not always accepting the marketing hyperbole created by the organization. This was typical of most of his former colleagues, he said. The other group was much smaller and perhaps scarier. These were the "true believers," as he put it, who saw credit rating as a science and were relentless in their determination that rating be at the heart of the financial markets. True believers, he implied, were trouble. From this I read they lacked healthy skepticism and were less inclined to place emphasis on the character of ratings as no more than opinions.

Typically, people think about credit ratings as having some explicit behavioral effect on the issuer of the rated debt. Ratings that are lower than desired may force the issuer to offer higher interest to sell all their securities. This more expensive credit reduces the resources they have available for other uses. Another way to think about ratings is indirectly or nonbehaviorally. The focus here is on the issuer anticipating the reaction of the rating agencies. Issuers act in advance of this to change themselves and what they do in ways that might be agreeable to the agencies, hopefully securing a better rating.

Looked at this way, ratings are much more consequential things than they appear behaviorally. They can be likened to federal funding programs in the United States that are conditional on policy change at the state and local level. A nonbehavioral or structural approach, when the vast sums of money at stake are taken into consideration, clarifies the potentially enormous significance of rating. Like credit card debt for the individual, ratings provide a disciplinary force on institutions that can change what they do and how they operate. Unlike law, or the pronouncements of politicians, this form of discipline is covert and unaccountable.[13]

The Rating Process

In recent years, the credit rating process has become a thing to be feared and wondered about. The assumption, it seems, is that there is something secretive and occult about the rating process, akin to Masonic ritual. A lot has been written about how to do well in this process and thus secure a better rating than might otherwise be the case.[14] The agencies have provided more information about, and discussion of, the process over the past thirty years. In broad terms, the process brings together quantitative information about the debt and income circumstances of the issuer, and qualitative information about their business prospects, industry circumstances, and management. Because ratings meld quantitative and qualitative information, they are products of human judgment. Ratings of this sort cannot be a simple "reading" of data.

Once the analyst has gathered data, which typically includes confidential information provided by the issuer relating to business plans, she develops a report and recommendation subject to managerial oversight. This is deliberated on by a rating committee. The

---

13. On this form of power, see Susan Strange, *States and Markets* (London: Pinter, 1988); Peter Miller and Nikolas Rose, "Governing Economic Life," *Economy and Society* 19, no. 1 (1990): 1–31; and Bartholomew Paudyn, *Credit Ratings and Sovereign Debt: The Political Economy of Creditworthiness through Risk and Uncertainty* (Basingstoke: Palgrave Macmillan, 2014).

14. See, for example, Langohr and Langohr, *The Rating Agencies and Their Credit Ratings.*

committees are crucial because this is where data meets experience, and the views of relatively junior officials can be assessed by senior staff. It is the rating committees that produce the rating. The rating agencies do not divulge what happens in rating committees, just as in the judicial system in most developed countries jury deliberations are secret, and as the records of these committees are destroyed like other business records after a few years, there are no historical archives of rating committee decisions for scholars to peruse.[15] Unlike with jury deliberations, rating agencies do provide a written rationale for ratings, which have become more elaborate as the rating system has become subject to greater criticism since the Enron scandal. A key issue debated in recent years is the fact that issuers pay the rating agencies to produce ratings.

Like other institutions, the rating agencies and their staffers do not approach the world without their own preconceived ideas about matters of import to them, including what is creditworthy. Contrary to the expectations of some, the agencies approach creditworthiness in a pragmatic way. Consciously, they say they are trying to defend and promote the interests of investors. This is the keystone of their worldview. So, what do their principals want and need? Uncertainty seems to be the paramount enemy and what the agencies are focused on transforming into risk.[16] This, of course, makes sense given the prevalence of a risk/uncertainty dichotomy in modern

---

15. The only public discussion of the activities and records of these rating agency committees can be found in reports by the US Securities and Exchange Commission, such as *Summary Report of Issues Identified in the Commission Staff's Examinations of Select Credit Rating Agencies*, July 2008, https://www.sec .gov/files/craexamination070808.pdf, accessed March 3, 2016.

16. Rawi Abdelal and Mark Blyth, "Just Who Put You in Charge? We Did: CRAs and the Politics of Ratings," in *Ranking the World: Grading States as a Tool of Global Governance*, ed. Alexander Cooley and Jack Snyder, 39–59 (Cambridge: Cambridge University Press, 2015), 54.

thinking about finance.[17] Uncertainty is the enemy because it cannot be quantified, because uncertainty cannot be specified in terms of loss. What investors need is a sense of what their money will buy them in terms of return, and of course, the risk of loss that comes with this income. That risk is specified in terms of probability. Probability here is delineated in terms of a point on the rating scale. Given this, the rating agencies do not react well to poor communications from issuers, deception, or lack of full disclosure. So, transparency is a key rating agency expectation of securities issuers.

Agencies seem to want issuers that respond to their requests for information, that communicate effectively, that are not evasive, that try to be helpful, that treat the agencies well. One way to characterize this is that issuers behave based on an implicit recognition of their standing not as principals but as agents in the rating process.[18] Their job, as agents, is to provide the agencies (who are also agents, but of the investors) with the information they need to do their job. Issuers run into problems with the agencies when they start to see themselves as principals, when they see their interests as being what the rating agencies should be striving to serve. If issuers can work out—from the point of view of the agencies—that it is the investors who are the people to be served in this relationship, they will understand better the dynamics of their relationship with the rating agencies.

From my conversations with agency officials, it became clear that in the case of government bonds, rating agencies do not want to see general taxation sources committed to the repayment of these

---

17. A key text in the development of this way of thinking is Frank H. Knight, *Risk, Uncertainty and Profit* (Washington, DC: Beard Books, 2002 [1921]).

18. On principals and agents, see John W. Pratt and Richard J. Zeckhauser, *Principals and Agents: The Structure of Business* (Boston: Harvard Business School Press, 1991).

bonds wherever possible. Taxation is a public process, built on political power. Like all political processes it is subject to the struggle
between interests. Taxation is also highly variable in volume given
the upswings and the downswings of economic life. In good times,
taxation can produce strong revenues for a local council or a national government. In bad times, taxation revenues diminish. Given
this, and given the aversion of the agencies to uncertainty, what they
are eager to do is tie sources of revenue to repayment of debt issues wherever possible. This preference creates a bias toward proj-
ects that are self-funding, like toll roads and other revenue-generating
investments.

If we examine each rating decision discretely, we can argue about
their merits or lack thereof. What is hidden in this analysis are the
broader consequences of rating, in terms of their effect on the scope
of thinking and action of issuers and investors alike. In Britain, until
recently, individuals seeking accommodation merely needed a letter from their employer to verify their income. This system changed
to one more recognizable to Americans, in which individuals have
personal credit ratings, around 2000. This meant that individuals,
like issuers of debt securities, had to be more mindful of aspects of
their financial life than they had in the past. The sense of being
monitored, of being watched, develops over time. In earlier work,
I have argued that the apprehension of being monitored on the part
of issuers is part of the structural power of rating. At a concrete and
practical level that structural power translates into what we might
call a private form of public policy, where the rating agencies are
those making policy and the issuers are those attempting to implement it.[19]

---

19. Timothy J. Sinclair, "Between State and Market: Hegemony and Institutions of Collective Action under Conditions of International Capital Mobility,"

This implicit public policy, pursued by private agents, shapes the choices made both by private sector and government issuers of debt securities. The emphasis on verification, on risk as opposed to uncertainty, on adopting the norms of an industry, puts private seekers of debt funding in the position where they must substantiate their claims. While this might be a very good thing, one could interpret this as inserting new levels of rational planning, or bureaucratization, into business life. The implicit public policy here could be thought to produce a highly rationalized administrative form of capitalism, other things being equal.[20]

Financial Disintermediation

The dynamism of finance is central to understanding what rating agencies have done and why they have done these things. The traditional institutions at the heart of finance have changed, and with that change has come new roles for the agencies, and new opportunities for them to make choices. This new global finance has destabilized the previously dominant norms of the agencies, shifting them onto a synchronic track, changing them from disinterested observers to keen participants in finance, a change from which many problems have arisen.

In traditional—fractional reserve—banking, the assets of the bank are the loans the banks make that earn the bank interest payments from borrowers. The liabilities of the bank are the deposits

---

Policy Sciences 27, no. 4 (1994): 447–466. On structural power, also see Susan Strange, *The Retreat of the State: The Diffusion of Power in the World Economy* (Cambridge: Cambridge University Press, 1996), 25–27.

20. As discussed by James Burnham, *The Managerial Revolution* (New York: John Day, 1941); also see Adolf Berle and Gardiner C. Means, *The Modern Corporation and Private Property* (New York: Macmillan, 1932).

held by customers in the bank. Deposits are liabilities because they can be withdrawn at any moment and earn no income for the bank. To make money and cover their costs, banks hold reserves that are only a fraction of their total deposits. This mismatch between the long-term assets of banks in the form of loans, and their short-term liabilities in the form of deposits, is known as the maturity transformation problem. Maturity transformation is what makes banks potentially profitable but also vulnerable to bank runs and collapse. If enough customers show up at the counter wanting to withdraw their money, the bank will not be able to cover all withdrawals because much of this money has been lent to customers in an effort to earn interest income. More money has been lent to customers than is available quickly to depositors should depositors want all their funds. Banks have traditionally gone to a lot of trouble to create the impression of solidity to assuage depositor anxiety about their solvency, often housing themselves in modern re-creations of Greek and Roman temples. Intermediating between depositors and those who borrow costs banks money. Bank intermediation must absorb the costs of bad loans made by the bank in the past. Other things equal, borrowers pay for bad loans by paying an interest rate that covers these liabilities on bank balance sheets, plus the overhead costs of bank staff, their pensions, and everything else.

For many borrowers, bank intermediation remains a quick and effective way of getting the money they need. Potential borrowers do not have to seek out lenders or investors. They can just go to a bank, which serves as intermediary between borrowers and lenders. However, in recent years, depositors have found more attractive things to do with their money at the same time as borrowers have increasingly borrowed from nonbank sources. The reasons for this development seem to lie in the heightened competitive pressures generated by globalization, and the high overhead costs of bank intermediation. Disintermediation is changing what banks are, creating an "information problem" for suppliers and users of funds. In a bank-intermediated environment, lenders depend on the prudential behavior of banks, which are required to maintain a certain level of reserves. Borrowing from banks is less competitive today as cheaper alternatives to banks exist. Borrowers such as corporations and governments have increasingly sought funds in the capital markets, where costs do not include the cost of running a bank and its infrastructure, and the bad loans the bank has made in the past.

Unsurprisingly, disintermediation is most advanced in the United States, where the rating agencies originate.[21] The process has accelerated in Europe since the early 1990s, with disintermediation in Asia being spurred by the poor performance of local banks in the Asian financial crisis of the late 1990s. In the United States, debt securities as a percentage of total corporate debt grew from 36 percent in 2008 to 50 percent in 2013. Banks maintain a 61 percent share of corporate debt funding in Europe, but this is down from 69 percent in 2008. In China, where finance is dominated by state-owned enterprises, capital markets have a 6 percent share, up from 4 percent in 2009.

Disintermediation has put the balance sheets of banks under pressure. Only less creditworthy borrowers will borrow from banks, as they cannot raise money on capital markets at lower cost than via the banking system. This increases the cost of intermediation and lowers returns, making traditional lending even less profitable. This dynamic, which ratchets down creditworthiness, threatens the existence of banking as we have known it since the late Middle Ages.

---

21. John Authers, "Incredible Shrinking of Banks as Clients Go Elsewhere," *Financial Times*, June 23, 2014, 14. Also see Standard & Poor's Rating Services, *Banking Disintermediation in Europe—A Slow-Growing Trend*, October 12, 2015, www.standardandpoors/ratingsdirect, accessed April 23, 2017.

Banks have responded to this process by trying to get into lucrative lines of business such as advising on mergers and acquisitions, and the creation and trading of complex new financial securities.[22] At the heart of the global financial crisis was an effort on the part of banks to use financial innovation to outlive their increasingly anachronistic role in lending to wholesale borrowers. As Authers notes, "The western world has suffered a long trail of financial crises that owe much to the after-effects of banks losing business lines to the capital markets."[23] As we will see in chapter 4, disintermediated funding takes on a new, little understood, and much faster-paced form in the years prior to the crisis.

The Rating Market in the Twenty-First Century

Beginning in the mid-1990s, credit rating agencies were increasingly accused of rating failures.[24] Episodes include the Orange County bankruptcy of 1994, the Asian financial crisis of 1997–1998, and the Enron bankruptcy of 2001. The accusations that the agencies had made mistakes about these ratings, had issued inflated ratings, or had not adequately investigated the circumstances of the

---

22. On this phenomenon, see Lena Rethel and Timothy J. Sinclair, *The Problem with Banks* (London: Zed, 2012).

23. Authers, "Incredible Shrinking of Banks," 14.

24. For history of the agencies, see Bruce G. Carruthers, "From Uncertainty toward Risk: The Case of Credit Ratings," *Socio-Economic Review* 11 (2013): 525–551; Marc Flandreau, Norbert Gaillard, and Frank Packer, "To Err Is Human: US Rating Agencies and the Interwar Foreign Government Debt Crisis," *European Review of Economic History* 15 (April 2011): 495–538; also see Marc Flandreau and Gabriel Geisler Mesevage, "The Separation of Information and Lending and the Rise of the Rating Agencies in the USA (1841–1907)," *Scandinavian Economic History Review* 62, no. 3 (2014): 213–242; and Daniel Cash, *The Role of the Credit Rating Agencies in Responsible Finance* (Basingstoke, UK: Palgrave Macmillan, 2018), 47–52.

issuers concerned come on top of years of complaints in the financial press about the backward-looking nature of ratings, the lack of timeliness of ratings, the outdatedness of ratings, and the inability of ratings to look forward.

The Enron crisis was perhaps the most telling rating failure. The problem with Enron was that it was engaged in very sophisticated financial engineering. The failure on the part of Andersen to detect fraud in Enron's accounts led to Arthur Andersen eventually surrendering its license to audit in 2002. The claim was that Andersen was motivated to give Enron a pass on its audit so that Andersen could secure lucrative consulting work.[25] The failure of the rating agencies to detect the fraudulent activity of Enron led to the first major effort to regulate the rating agencies in the United States.

Prior to the mid-1990s, the rating industry could be described as a comfortable duopoly. Moody's and S&P had most of the market to themselves. While there were other rating agencies, such as Dominion Bond Rating Service in Toronto, or Duff and Phelps in Chicago, these organizations had tiny percentages of the market and did not compete with Moody's and S&P in any meaningful way. A key development in the 1990s is the recapitalization of Fitch. Fitch had been around since 1913 but had come and gone as a serious player. In the mid-1990s this changed after a merger between IBCA in London and Fitch in New York, promoted by French interests. The new capital injected into the business led to greater ambition on the part of Fitch to secure market share. In the mid-1990s Fitch was a tiny outfit with a few employees in New York. Today, Fitch employees over two thousand people in thirty offices around

---

25. Although Andersen no longer provides auditing and accounting services, Andersen Consulting changed its name to Accenture in January 2001 and continues to operate.

the world. Fitch has gone from being a marginal player to being one of the so-called Big Three. The fact that we can refer to a Big Three reflects the greatly enhanced position of Fitch. Fitch's return to the big time shook up the rating market in the twenty-first century. The comfortable arrangement in which investors would secure two ratings, typically from Moody's and S&P, and very occasionally from one of the second-tier rating agencies, was disrupted. Now Moody's, S&P, and Fitch were in competition for those two slots, as had not been the case before. So, the rating industry from the late 1990s onward is not just more volatile in the sense that the financial markets are more volatile; it is more volatile because there is more internal competition and there are more resources to support competition.

A key feature of the traditional image of the rating industry is distance between the rating agencies and the issuers they rate. While the customers of the agencies are the issuers in the sense that it is issuers who pay for ratings, it was traditional within the agencies to regard investors as their true customers or principals. This led to a certain arm's-length character to the relationship between the rating agencies and the issuers of debt securities. The distance is exactly what the market expected of the agencies. This is the traditional model of rating. If you think about a professor grading the work of her students, you want that professor to have a certain critical distance from the students and not to have such a personal relationship with those students that she is unable to grade them objectively because she is compromised by her interactions with them. And it is precisely that objectivity, that distance, and that willingness to judge which the market expected the rating agencies to provide. Certainly, investors sought this quality from Moody's and S&P. Indeed, this is precisely the demeanor Moody's and to a lesser extent S&P had right up to the late 1990s: distance, objectivity, coolness, and aloofness. These are all part of the critical distance necessary to be able to issue judgments without fear or favor.

This critical distance, which I see as part of the diachronic position of the agencies in the financial markets, narrows greatly in the second half of the 1990s. The agencies become much more interested in what the market thinks of them. They start to ask the market what the market wants. The Enron debacle accelerates this process. At the same time, greater market utilization of RMBS increases the complexity of financial instruments in the markets. Securitized debt is organized in a hierarchy of tranches. Higher tranches, with prior claims on the stream of revenue from the underlying mortgage lending, get higher ratings. So, ratings were essential to these emerging high-return securities. But the complexity of these instruments meant they were not transparent. This lack of transparency led to active advice giving by the rating agencies in the construction of these financial instruments. So, rather than the agencies providing what they normally did, which was a rating on something presented to them just prior to going to market, now they were involved in the financial engineering themselves, in the sense that they were providing information that was helping to actually construct and modify these financial instruments at creation.

This is a key moment because it means the rating agencies give up some of their distance as they increasingly behave as if they are consultancies that provide advice about how to get a better rating. What we see here is the transformation of a key part of the market infrastructure from a judgmental function into one that becomes about active construction of financial assets of specific creditworthiness. Even if the rating agencies implicitly had an active construction role before, in the sense that their criteria for ratings were known and could be anticipated by issuers, what we see with RMBS is a move from that passive, implicit role to one of active creation. It is as if the judge has got down from the bench in the courthouse and has started to assist the defense attorney in building her client's case. It is at this point that we can say that not only are the markets synchronic, but so are the gatekeepers. The gatekeepers are no longer playing the diachronic role, being conservative and offering a second view, but are actively involved in the organization of the market itself.

After the Credit Rating Agency Reform Act of 2006, the US Securities and Exchange Commission (SEC) approved several new nationally recognized statistical rating organizations (NRSROs). Prior to this, there were just a handful of NRSROs, dominated of course by Moody's, S&P, and Fitch, but after the act, with the creation of explicit criteria for the approval of NRSROs, and an application process, the SEC agreed to recognize a number of new NRSROs. In addition, in Germany, China, and Russia we see the emergence of new rating agencies. The rating agencies in China and Russia are particularly vocal in saying they exist in counterpoint to the US agencies and will be different from those agencies in fundamental respects. Even within the United States we see the emergence of small agencies such as Kroll Ratings. Strangely, the rating business for the start-ups does not seem to be such a lucrative thing. While the barriers to entry are no longer great in terms of government intervention in the United States, they do seem to be substantial in terms of market acceptance. Instead of the US rating market being transformed by the arrival of new agencies such as those from Japan and Canada, this does not happen. The minor agencies do not become significant players in the rating market. Their future viability remains unclear.

Regulation of the Rating Agencies

For most of the existence of the rating agencies they have not been regulated by government in any country. They came into being in the absence of government-provided information. Their role could be interpreted as complementary to the financial press. Within a little more than a decade, ratings were used by government agencies as benchmarks to regulate the behavior of pension funds. Formally and informally, this role continues to the present.[26] For government agencies, ratings were dynamic and cheap, and so it is no wonder they piggybacked on this privately generated market information. The alternative would have meant creating a substitute. But as ratings had already achieved widespread use, especially in the US municipal market during the 1920s, it must have seemed very appropriate to take advantage of these new sources of judgment. For many pension funds the use of ratings established a division between investment-grade ratings and speculative grade. From 1936, US banks were able to invest in investment-grade but not speculative-grade bonds.[27] This meant that when ratings fell below investment-grade the institutions had to sell their assets. In this example, the use of ratings in prudential regulation creates a cliff edge situation, which in the context of financial problems can lead to behavior that is pro-cyclical—making a financial panic worse— because the banks suddenly have to sell assets that are no longer investment-grade.

Until the 1980s, most corporate ratings were of blue-chip or very financially sound corporations. The junk bond or high yield market did not exist. Credit ratings were held by municipalities and by deep-pocketed private entities. Rating was not a highly innovative business, and the securities business was not highly innovative

---

26. On using ratings in the regulation of financial institutions, see Timothy J. Sinclair, *The New Masters of Capital: American Bond Rating Agencies and the Politics of Creditworthiness* (Ithaca, NY: Cornell University Press, 2005), 42–49.

27. Lawrence J. White, "The Credit Rating Agencies," *Journal of Economic Perspectives* 24, no. 2 (Spring 2010): 213.

either. Rating agencies were conservative, diachronic organizations. The agencies were not there to make the life of bond market participants easier. They were there as gatekeepers, as part of the architecture of the markets. The agencies represented a different ethos, and everybody knew it. The problems created by using the outputs of the rating agencies in regulation only becomes evident at the end of the 1980s. What changes is that finance is transformed from the conservatism of the Bretton Woods era, focused on the creation of productive enterprises, to the innovation of the post–Bretton Woods world. In finance, this means much greater variegation of the creditworthiness of those seeking funding from the securities markets. The municipalities and blue-chip companies that dominated the securities issuing business between World War I and the 1970s were now rivaled by speculators that engaged in mergers and acquisitions, sometimes premised on leveraged buyouts. These new financial actors were interested in obtaining cheap funding from the securities markets. Michael Milken, of Drexel Burnham Lambert, argued that ratings did not accurately capture the value of less financially strong organizations. Although the rating agencies resisted the rise of the junk bond market in the 1980s, its arrival represents a sea change for them. In future, they would be rating a more diverse universe of credits.

The notion of a nationally recognized statistical rating organization or NRSRO emerges in 1975 with a new rule created by the Securities and Exchange Commission. This new rule, the net capital rule, was intended to ensure that broker-dealers had enough financial resources to cover their obligations if they got into difficulty. Within this new rule broker-dealers could reduce their liquidity requirement by purchasing securities of investment-grade rated by an NRSRO. Although it sounds well developed, the notion of an NRSRO was very simple. The designation was possible only

TABLE 2

EU and US Regulation of Rating Agencies

Year	EU/US	Name and Details
1975	US	*SEC, Rule 15c3-1 (the net capital rule)* was an amendment to the Securities Exchange Act of 1934 that allowed brokers to reduce the liquidity they were required to hold if securities were rated by a Nationally Recognized Statistical Rating Organization. The characteristics of NRSROs were not defined, and the SEC issued "no action" letters to established US agencies. The NRSRO concept was subsequently used by Congress in a wide range of financial legislation.
1994–97	US	SEC proposed codifying what defined an NRSRO and creating an NRSRO determination process in a 1994 concept release and a 1997 rule proposal. These proposals were driven by the professional staff in the SEC and were not strongly supported by the SEC commissioners nor considered by Congress.
2002	US	*Sarbanes-Oxley Act (section 702).* This Enron-inspired legislation required the SEC to conduct a study of the role and functions of the credit rating agencies in the securities markets with attention to accuracy, barriers to entry, conflicts of interest, and measures that might improve performance. The SEC delivered this report to a Senate committee in January 2003.
2004	EU	*MiFID Directive (2004/39/EC).* This required agencies to specify that their ratings are opinions, not recommendations to invest, and required agencies to disclose potential conflicts of interest that occurred during the rating process.
2006	US	*Credit Rating Agency Reform Act.* This is the first substantial legislative measure to regulate the agencies. It focuses on conflicts of interest within agency staff, creates the Office of Rating Agencies within the SEC to monitor the agencies, and codifies the process for determining what an NRSRO is and how to become one. This legislation did not challenge either the analytical or business model of the agencies.

(continued)

TABLE 2
(*continued*)

Year	EU/US	Name and Details
2006	EU	*Capital Requirements Directives (2006/48/EC & 2006/49/ EC)*. This directive enacted features of Basel II, establishing a list of recognized agencies like the NRSRO concept.
2009	EU	*Regulation (EC) No. 1060/2009 ("CRA I")*. Based on European Commission proposals, this legislation sought to avoid conflicts of interest, ban consultancy to rated entities, scrutinize models and processes, increase transparency and internal controls, and establish registration and surveillance frameworks. This legislation did not challenge either the analytical or business model of the agencies.
2010	US	*Dodd-Frank Wall Street Reform and Consumer Protection Act (Title IX, Subtitle C)*. Sec. 939G imposed SEC Rule 436(g) on the agencies, removing their First Amendment rights and exposing them to liability as experts for error. The act also mandated that a series of reports be written on the agencies, and marginally tweaked the provisions of the Credit Rating Agency Reform Act. Aside from Sec. 939G, this legislation did not challenge either the analytical or business model of the agencies.
2011	US	*Asset-Backed Market Stabilization Act*. This one-page act repealed section 939G of the Dodd-Frank Act. Repeal of this provision restored First Amendment protection to ratings, freeing the agencies from the application of SEC Rule 436(g), which exposed the agencies to liability for material misstatements and omissions related to rating.
2011	EU	*Regulation (EC) No. 513/2011 ("CRA II")*. This adds to CRA I by giving the newly established European Securities and Markets Authority (ESMA) the status of sole supervisor in the EU over rating agencies. This legislation did not challenge either the analytical or business model of the agencies.
2013	EU	*Regulation (EU) No. 462/2013 ("CRA III")*. Excessive reliance on ratings by investors was the target of this measure. This legislation did not seriously challenge either the analytical or business model of the agencies.

Sources: Various SEC documents; author's field work; Mennillo and Sinclair 2019; Olivier Nataf, Lieven De Moor, and Rosanne Vanpée, "Was Regulation (EC) No 1060/2009 on Credit Rating Agencies Effective?," *Journal of Bank Regulation* 19 (2018): 300–302, 312.

for those credit rating agencies recognized by the markets. At the time this included Moody's, S&P, and, with less foundation, Fitch. There was no application process, and so there was no obvious way to become an NRSRO. For thirty years after the passage of this rule the SEC issued what have come to be known as "no action" letters to those it deemed to have NRSRO standing. Given the only way to be an NRSRO was to be already recognized nationally, it put new agencies and foreign agencies that wanted to do business in the United States in an impossible position. Critics came to see the NRSRO designation as a barrier to entry that created an ossified rent-seeking rating industry in the United States.[28] If new entrants could not become NRSROs, this put incumbents in a position where they could charge exorbitant fees and provide whatever quality product they determined, free of any meaningful market constraint.

The Enron scandal and bankruptcy of late 2001 brought to a head a decade and a half of quiet market unhappiness about the credit rating agencies. Enron was a major energy company based in Houston, Texas. It engaged in extraordinary financial innovation. Kenneth Lay, CEO of Enron, was subsequently found guilty of ten counts of securities fraud.[29] The scandal and bankruptcy led to the passing of the Sarbanes-Oxley Act in 2002, which required accounting firms to focus on accounting and auditing and to give up their consultancy and other businesses such as law firms. Although the credit rating agencies were not directly complicit like Andersen, the degree to which the agencies took information from issuers rather than generating information themselves became evident. Hearings

---

28. Frank Partnoy, "The Siskel and Ebert of Financial Markets? Two Thumbs Down for the Credit Rating Agencies," *Washington University Law Quarterly* 77, no. 3 (1999): 619–712.

29. Lay died in 2006 before he could be sentenced. His convictions were subsequently canceled.

were held in Congress, and in time the first act to directly regulate the agencies emerged. This law, the Credit Rating Agency Reform Act, was enacted September 2006. Despite its title, this is a very modest law. Its focus was on reforming the NRSRO process. For the first time, there would be a recognized means through which new providers of credit ratings could apply to become an NRSRO. This would occur via a new Office of Credit Ratings to be established in the SEC. This new law did not challenge the funding system that underpinned the rating agencies. Nor did the rating agency reform act attempt to intervene in the analysis or determination of credit ratings.

More than a decade on from passage of the reform act, eight NRSROs are recognized by the SEC. The SEC administers the process for applying to become, and maintain, NRSRO status. The staff of the SEC generate an annual report on the NRSRO system that covers basic facts and implications for competition and transparency. The new system has overcome the key constraint that characterized the old system. It has proven possible for some new rating agencies to be recognized. This is true even of agencies that are located outside of the United States, including one in Canada and two in Japan. However, there is clearly an inner core and an outer rim among rating agencies. All the new agencies recognized are niche players in the ratings business. None of them offer mainline competition to the Big Three rating agencies. Nor does the NRSRO process challenge the established business model or analytical procedures of Moody's, S&P, and Fitch. Given this, it is not clear that the revamped NRSRO process has made any substantial difference to the fundamental characteristics of the credit rating industry.

Within a couple of years of passage of this law, the rating agencies were embroiled in the worst rating crisis up to that time. Given that the focus of the reform act is not on rating analysis or the incentives in the rating agency business model, it seems best to conclude that the reforms in the act were either irrelevant or marginal to rating agency performance in the germination of the crisis. If we put the global financial crisis to one side, it is hard to make a case that the act brought any meaningful reform. Counterintuitively, the strongest implication of the act has been to shore up the position of the Big Three by creating a public accountability framework for what they do. This provides the agencies with cover from more substantive reforms that would address their business models and analytical procedures. The Dodd-Frank Wall Street Reform and Consumer Protection Act has, however, taxed the agencies. They spend a lot of time and money meeting the requirements for reporting, as they have told me when I have discussed regulation with them in New York and London.[30] But placing costs on the agencies and creating public accountability does not mean that real substantive change has occurred. In fact, the best assessment may be that Dodd-Frank assists the agencies in defending themselves from criticism more than anything else.

The Dodd-Frank Act became law when signed by President Obama on July 21, 2010. The act is voluminous at 848 published pages. It contains measures to address the rating agencies at Title IX, Subtitle C, "Improvements to the Regulation of Credit Rating Agencies." The legislation identifies the central role of the agencies in "capital formation, investor confidence and the efficient performance of the United States economy."[31] This leads to measures in the act to create mechanisms

---

30. This is one of the points made by Ian Linnell, global analytical head, Fitch Ratings, Canary Wharf, London, October 2, 2014. These compliance costs are also noted by Matthew P. Richardson, Marti G. Subrahmanyam, Laura L. Veldkamp, and Lawrence J. White, "Credit Rating Agencies and the Financial CHOICE Act," in *Regulating Wall Street: CHOICE Act vs. Dodd-Frank*, ed. Matthew P. Richardson, Kermit L. Schoenholtz, Bruce Tuckman, and Lawrence J. White (New York: Center for Global Economy and Business, New York University Stern School of Business, 2017), 168.

31. Dodd-Frank Act, p. 497.

for "public oversight and accountability, standards of liability and concerns about conflict of interest."[32] Importantly, in Dodd-Frank conflicts of interest are deemed to be related to personnel issues, not to the business model. Dodd-Frank did precipitate the removal of ratings from federal law, where they had become de facto standards since the 1930s. Bank regulators eliminated references and reliance on ratings by 2012–2013, and the SEC did the same for money market mutual funds in September 2015, but the US Department of Labor was still making use of ratings in 2017.[33] State regulators of insurance, not covered by Dodd-Frank, have not eliminated reliance on ratings.[34]

Al Franken, the colorful US senator from Minnesota (2009–2018), crafted an amendment to Dodd-Frank mandating a ratings board to be housed in the SEC's Office of Credit Ratings. This board would assign rating agencies to issuers, rather than allow issuers to choose which rating agency to employ. The idea was to break the cash nexus between issuers and raters, eliminating the conflict of interest in the issuer-pays business model.[35] But Franken's amendment did not survive in this form into the law. Instead, Dodd-Frank

---

32. Ginevra Marandola and Timothy J. Sinclair, "Credit Rating Agencies Are Poorly Understood and the Rules Developed for Them Will Not Work," *Handbook of the Geographies of Money and Finance*, ed. Jane Pollard and Ron Martin (London: Edward Elgar, 2017), 22. Also see Norbert J. Gaillard and Michael Waibel, "The Icarus Syndrome: How Credit Rating Agencies Lost Their Quasi Immunity," *SMU Law Review* 71, no. 4 (Fall 2018): 1077–1116. Despite the Asset-Backed Market Stabilization Act of 2011, Gaillard and Waibel argue that since the agencies started to rate structured finance issues, rating has become more advisory in character, and courts have responded by eroding their First Amendment rights. See Gaillard and Waibel, "The Icarus Syndrome," 1080–1081.

33. Richardson et al., "Credit Rating Agencies and the Financial CHOICE Act," 169–170.

34. Richardson et al., 170.

35. Richardson et al., 171.

required the SEC to study Franken's idea.[36] The SEC staff report, published in December 2012, did not strongly endorse the Franken model, and the idea went no further.[37]

A bold but ultimately doomed element of Title IX, Subtitle C was Section 939G, which removed the protection of Rule 436(g) of the Securities Act of 1933 from the rating agencies. Rule 436(g) exempted NRSROs "from liability as 'experts' under Section 11 of that Act."[38] Based on an earlier concept release by the SEC, this would remove the agencies' First Amendment rights to offer opinions (like all US citizens) and impose on them new liabilities when their ratings were included on Asset-Backed Security (ABS) registration statements. The provision had, apparently, "garnered little attention" prior to passage of the law.[39]

But Congress had not reckoned on the rating agencies. The agencies refused to allow their ratings to be used for ABS filings, bringing that market to a halt overnight. The SEC immediately provided temporary relief from enforcement of the provision, extending that reprieve indefinitely on November 23, 2010. The background to this development is that the agencies' First Amendment protection had been challenged in

36. Marc Joffe, "Congress Should Open the Door to Not-for-Profit Credit Rating Agencies," *Oxford Business Law Blog*, March 2, 2018, https://www.law.ox .ac.uk/business-law-blog/blog/2018/03/congress-should-open-door-not-profit -credit-rating-agencies, September 2, 2020.

37. U.S. Securities and Exchange Commission, *Report to Congress on Assigned Credit Ratings, as Required by Section 939F of the Dodd-Frank Wall Street Reform and Consumer Protection Act* (Washington, DC: US Securities and Exchange Commission, December 2012).

38. James Morphy, "SEC Amends Rules Related to Credit Rating Agencies," December 10, 2009, https://corpgov.law.harvard.edu/2009/12/10/sec-amends-rules -related-to-credit-rating-agencies/, accessed April 16, 2017.

39. Steven G. Bordy and Cynthia Hanawalt, "Dodd-Frank: Rating Agencies and the ABS Market," *Law360*, January 24, 2011, https://www.morganlewis.com /-/media/files/docs/archive/dodd-frank-rating-agencies-and-the-abs-market _6247pdf.ashx, accessed September 14, 2020.

recent years in court decisions. In particular, on September 2, 2009, Judge Shira Scheindlin of the Southern District of New York, in *Abu Dhabi Commercial Bank v. Morgan Stanley & Co.*, rejected

> the argument that rating opinions were entitled to immunity under the First Amendment. Judge Scheindlin acknowledged that "it is well-established that under typical circumstances, the First Amendment protects rating agencies, subject to an 'actual malice' exception, from liability arising out of their issuance of ratings and reports because their ratings are considered matters of public concern." However, she distinguished that generalized protection for ratings disseminated to the public at large from situations where ratings are provided only to a select group of investors, explaining that, in those narrower circumstances, the ratings do not warrant First Amendment protection.[40]

A subsequent ruling in California, in the case of *California Public Employees' Retirement Systems v. Moody's Corp. et al.* in 2010, cited the New York ruling and widened the removal of First Amendment rights because, said the judge,

> the right to free speech allows us to give our opinions on things of public concern. The issuance of these SIV [structured investment vehicle] ratings is not, however, an issue of public concern. Rather, it is an economic activity designed for a limited target for the purpose of making money. That is not something that should be afforded First Amendment protection and the defendants are not akin to members of the financial press.[41]

The SEC had contemplated Rule 436(g) repeal for some time and sought industry comment in September 2009.[42] The agencies sent

---

40. Bordy and Hanawalt, 1.
41. Quoted in Bordy and Hanawalt, 2.
42. *Annual Report on Nationally Recognized Statistical Rating Organizations* (Washington, DC: US Securities and Exchange Commission), September 2009, 21.

letters about the issue in December 2009 and met with the SEC in early 2010. At this point it appeared the agencies had fended off removal of their First Amendment rights. However, late in the Dodd-Frank reconciliation process

> the line was inserted into the Dodd-Frank Act by congresswoman Mary Jo Kilroy, a Democrat from Ohio whose stated goal was to increase the potential liability for credit rating agencies—her amendment to the conference committee bill was passed on June 16th while the House and Senate versions were being reconciled.
>
> Perhaps the repeal of Rule 436(g) went unremarked because the focal point for analysts was the potential shift in the entire NRSRO business model, a system that was under attack as the legislation was drafted but ultimately left untouched. Indeed, analysts concluded that the law's consequences for rating agencies were mild, particularly in contrast with the harsher impact they had anticipated.[43]

In response to this outcome, Fitch observed that

> Fitch is not willing to take on such liability without a complete understanding of the ramifications of that liability to Fitch's business and the means by which Fitch may be able to effectively mitigate the risks associated therewith. While Fitch will continue to publish credit ratings and research, given the potential consequences, Fitch cannot consent to including Fitch credit ratings in prospectuses and registration statements at this time.[44]

A planned new issue by Ford Motor Credit Company in July 2010 of $1.08 billion in securities backed by automobile loans is reportedly

---

43. Bordy and Hanawalt, "Dodd-Frank," 2.

44. "Fitch Comments on U.S. Financial Reform Act's Implication for Credit Rating Agencies," July 19, 2020, https://www.businesswire.com/news/home/2010071 9006158/en/Fitch-Comments-U.S.-Financial-Reform-Acts-Implication, accessed September 14, 2020.

what led to SEC action to freeze enforcement action of the Dodd-Frank provision.[45] Section 939G of Dodd-Frank was repealed by the Asset-Backed Market Stabilization Act of 2011, which became law in August that year. It is a very short act that does just this one thing. It gives the rating agencies back their First Amendment rights, as they enjoyed from the founding of Moody's in 1907. The only substantive effort to regulate the agencies following the global financial crisis, initiated by a lone congresswoman, ended in complete failure.

European efforts have been no more effective.[46] For many years rating agencies were little more than "recognized" by local regulators in European states, who were free riders on US regulation and scrutiny. With the onset of the global financial crisis European Commission officials have sought to regulate the agencies in Europe with proposed new laws passed by the European Parliament for referral to the Council of Ministers.[47] These efforts materialized in Regulation (EC) No. 1060/2009, on which the European legal framework for the regulation of rating agencies is based.[48] Since

---

45. Bordy and Hanawalt, "Dodd-Frank," 3.

46. This paragraph draws on Giulia Mennillo and Timothy J. Sinclair, "Global Financial Crises," in *Issues in 21st Century World Politics*, 3rd ed., ed. Mark Beeson and Nick Bisley (London: Palgrave Macmillan, 2017), 167. Also see Andreas Kruck, "Resilient Blunderers: Credit Rating Fiascos and Rating Agencies' Institutionalized Status as Private Authorities," *Journal of European Public Policy* 23, no. 5 (2016): 753–770.

47. European Parliament, Committee on Economic and Monetary Affairs, "Draft Report on the Proposal for a Regulation of the European Parliament and of the Council on Credit Rating Agencies," Strasbourg, January 13, 2009. Quaglia explains how the EU shifted to a more active approach to rating agency supervision and how the agencies lobbied to reduce the prescriptive nature of the new rules. Lucia Quaglia, "The Regulatory Response of the European Union to the Global Financial Crisis," in *Crisis and Control: Institutional Change in Financial Market Regulation*, ed. Renate Mayntz (Frankfurt: Campus Verlag, 2012), 180.

48. European Parliament, Council of the European Union, Regulation (EC) No. 1060/2009 of the European Parliament and of the Council of 16 Septem-

July 2011, the European Securities and Markets Authority, known as ESMA, has been the single supervisor over credit rating agencies in the European Union.[49] ESMA administers a registration process like the NRSRO system, addressing issues of competition, transparency, and disclosure in the rating process. But, like Dodd-Frank, it does not change rating analytics or effectively challenge the issuer-pays model of rating funding.[50]

F. Amtenbrink and J. De Haan question whether the regime under Regulation 1060/2009 in the EU will make "a decisive difference compared to the previously existing mix of regulation

---

ber 2009 on credit rating agencies (text with EEA relevance), OJ L 302, November 17, 2009.

49. European Parliament, Council of the European Union, Regulation (EU) No. 513/2011 of the European Parliament and of the Council of 11 May 2011 amending Regulation (EC) No. 1060/2009 on credit rating agencies (text with EEA relevance), OJ L 145, May 31, 2011. Also see European Parliament, Council of the European Union, Regulation (EU) No. 462/2013 of the European Parliament and of the Council of 21 May 2013 amending Regulation (EC) No. 1060/2009 on credit rating agencies (text with EEA relevance), OJ L 146, May 31, 2013a. Also see European Parliament, Council of the European Union, Directive 2013/14/EU of the European Parliament and of the Council of 21 May 2013 amending Directive 2003/41/EC on the activities and supervision of institutions for occupational retirement provision, Directive 2009/65/EC on the coordination of laws, regulations, and administrative provisions relating to undertakings for collective investment in transferable securities (UCITS), and Directive 2011/61/EU on Alternative Investment Funds Managers in respect of overreliance on credit ratings (text with EEA relevance), OJ L 145, May 31, 2013b.

50. Ian Linnell explained to me that although the merits of specific regulatory measures enacted in both the United States and the EU can be debated, one useful thing to come out of the recent reregulation of the rating agencies is an annual college of regulators that alternates between Paris and Washington, D.C., hosted by ESMA and the SEC, respectively. This event, which, as he described it to me, sounds remarkably like an academic colloquium, furthers the exchange of ideas between regulators, and between the regulators and the agencies. Interview with Ian Linnell, president of Fitch Ratings, Canary Wharf, London, September 22, 2020.

and self-regulation."[51] Dimitrios Soudis does not think the agencies have any independent impact, implying that regulating them would have little effect.[52] Amtenbrink and K. Heine argue that the legislative initiatives in the United States and the EU "aimed at increasing the regulatory oversight over credit rating agencies activities, where non-binding international standards and self-commitment were thought to have failed," are not a surprising "reaction to market failure."[53]

This "countermovement towards regulation" was predictable, they suggest. But the authors question whether registration and certification systems are "not in fact counterproductive." Insights from behavioral science suggest to them that public regulation triggers even "further overconfidence" in credit ratings and, accordingly, increases overreliance; "by introducing numerous measures geared towards increasing the quality and reliability of credit ratings, investors are not exactly discouraged from relying on ratings."[54]

Andreas Kruck is also concerned that regulation of rating agencies fosters reproduction of the credit rating agencies "as recognized and trustworthy private authority" and promotes the "progressive institutionalization . . . of their role as private governors."[55] Kruck notes how difficult it has been for US regulators to respond to the significant role of the agencies in US capital markets, given how embedded the agencies have become.[56] Rawi Abdelal and Mark Blyth

---

51. F. Amtenbrink and J. De Haan, "Credit Rating Agencies," DNB Working Papers, No. 278 (Netherlands Central Bank, Research Department, 2011), 33.

52. Soudis, "Credit Rating Agencies and the IPE," 830.

53. F. Amtenbrink and K. Heine, "Regulating Credit Rating Agencies in the European Union: Lessons from Behavioural Science," *Dovenschmidt Quarterly* 2, no. 1 (2013): 13.

54. Amtenbrink and Heine, 12.

55. Kruck, "Resilient Blunderers," 765, 754.

56. Andreas Kruck, "Asymmetry in Empowering and Disempowering Private Intermediaries: The Case of Credit Rating Agencies," *Annals of the American Academy of Political and Social Science* 670, no. 1 (2017): 135.

agree.[57] Stefano Pagliari argues that the regulatory change in Europe has reduced reliance on agents of market discipline such as the rating agencies.[58] Eric Helleiner and Hongying Wang argue that competition from new emerging market agencies is unlikely to challenge the entrenched US agencies.[59] Andreas Nölke interprets European efforts to regulate the agencies as part of a process of reducing "extreme volatility" in financial markets, suggesting that the agencies' actions are seen as making crises worse.[60]

Around the time Dodd-Frank became law, the Financial Stability Board (FSB) started an initiative to reduce reliance on the agencies' ratings.[61] This is depicted in table 3. The rationale behind this initiative is that reliance on ratings in regulatory requirements and investment standards triggers mechanistic market responses to rating changes. Especially in times of crisis, the FSB suggested, rating overreliance can translate into fire sales of securities under downward rating pressure and make crises worse. Consequently, if reliance on credit ratings in regulation is reduced, rating actions will be less consequential, and herd behavior less likely.

Compliance with the FSB principles has occurred among public agencies across much of the G20, although implementation has

57. Abdelal and Blyth, "Just Who Put You in Charge?," 59.

58. Stefano Pagliari, "Who Governs Finance? The Shifting Public-Private Divide in the Regulation of Derivatives, Rating Agencies and Hedge Funds," *European Law Journal* 18, no. 1 (2012): 44.

59. Eric Helleiner and Hongying Wang, "Limits to the BRICS' Challenge: Credit Rating Reform and Institutional Innovation in Global Finance," *Review of International Political Economy* 25, no. 5 (2018): 573.

60. Andreas Nölke, "Financialisation as the Core Problem for a 'Social Europe,'" *Revista de Economía Mundial* 46 (2017): 41.

61. This discussion of the FSB draws on Mennillo and Sinclair, "A Hard Nut to Crack," 266–286; Financial Stability Board, *Principles for Reducing Reliance on CRA Ratings*, (Basel, Switzerland: Financial Stability Board, 2010), https://www.fsb.org/wp-content/uploads/r_101027.pdf?page_moved=1, accessed July 6, 2017.

Table 3

Financial Stability Board Policy Work on Rating Agency Reform

Year	Measure
2008	*Report of the Financial Stability Forum on Enhancing Market and Institutional Resilience.* Section IV focused on reform of rating agencies. The report was critical of the quality of ratings, highlighting inadequate historical data and the use of flawed models. The report argued that conflicts of interest may be stronger in structured finance ratings, as the agencies are involved in designing the structuring. The report strongly recommended the agencies adequately resource expanding areas of work and review the quality of data input. The report warned of overreliance on ratings by investors and regulators.
2010	*Principles for Reducing Reliance on CRA Ratings* published October. This focused on usage by market participants and by regulators and central banks. Motivation was concern about herding and cliff-effects that arise from rating thresholds written into law and market practice.
2012	*Roadmap for Reducing Reliance on CRA Ratings* published November. The brief report identified steps to reduce regulatory reliance on ratings and to require financial institutions to create (or re-create) their own means of credit risk assessment.
2013	*Report to the G20 on Progress toward Reducing Reliance and Strengthening Oversight of the Credit Rating Agencies* and *Thematic Review of the FSB Principles for Reducing Reliance on CRA Ratings—Interim Report* published August. These were presented to the St. Petersburg G20 summit.
2014	*Thematic Review of the FSB Principles for Reducing Reliance on CRA Ratings—Final Report* published May. The report observes a lack of action toward FSB principles in many countries and comments on the challenges involved in creating new systems of credit risk assessment.

Sources: Adapted from https://www.fsb.org/policy_area/cras/ and https://www.fsb.org/work-of-the-fsb/implementation-monitoring/other-areas/.

been faster and more complete in the United States and the EU than elsewhere.[62] The FSB was critical of the slowness of the Basel Committee for Banking Supervision (BCBS) in removing ratings from the capital adequacy standards. It has proven more difficult to get those who work in the markets to abandon their use of the product of the rating agencies. More than a decade since the FSB's initiative began, a transformation of market utilization of ratings has not occurred. Evidence suggests reliance on credit rating agencies persists "particularly in private contracts, investment mandates, internal limits, and collateral agreements."[63] When the BCBS did present its revised Basel III (often called Basel IV) proposals to take ratings out of the capital adequacy process, market representatives opposed them.[64] The American Bankers Association underlined the international use, broad acceptance, and reluctance to abandon ratings among market participants.[65] The BCBS eventually introduced new norms for credit rating agencies to be used for the standardized approach to credit risk from 2022, but only in jurisdictions that continue to allow use of ratings for regulatory purposes.[66] These

62. Matthew Attwood, "FSB Demands Action on Credit Rating Agencies," *fn Financial News*, August 30, 2013, https://www.fnlondon.com/articles/fsb-demands-faster-action-on-ratings-agencies-20130830, accessed July 3, 2020.

63. Financial Stability Board, *Thematic Review on FSB Principles for Reducing Reliance on CRA Ratings—Peer Review Report*, May 12, 2014, 2, https://www.fsb.org/2014/05/r_140512/, accessed July 19, 2019. For an earlier, more critical assessment, see Francesco de Pascalis, "Reducing Overreliance on Credit Ratings: Failing Strategies and the Need to Start from Scratch," *Amicus Curiae* 91 (Autumn 2012): 17–21.

64. Sid Verma, "Bank Regulation: 'Basel IV' Sparks Banker Fury," *Euromoney*, March 5, 2015, https://www.euromoney.com/article/b12klgs5681h0r/bank-regulation-basel-iv-sparks-banker-fury, accessed July 19, 2019.

65. De Pascalis, "Reducing Overreliance on Credit Ratings," 20.

66. "Standardised Approach: Use of Credit Ratings," *Basel Framework*, December 15, 2019, https://www.bis.org/basel_framework/chapter/CRE/21.htm?inforce=20220101, accessed July 3, 2020.

norms are similar to the International Organization of Securities Commissions' (IOSCO) Code of Conduct Fundamentals for Credit Rating Agencies.[67]

Despite the public success of the FSB initiative in reducing official use of ratings, the widespread continued private market use of ratings should not be a surprise. Ratings are not technical things, like parts of your computer, that work or do not work. Nor is their manufacture something actually governed by national governments and their agencies. Market participants are happy to make up their own minds about ratings and argue for their use.[68] Reducing the credit rating agencies' authority in markets to a product of regulation has always been too simplistic an understanding of what they offer.

WHAT DO WE KNOW about the agencies? First, ratings are not what many people think they are. It turns out they are not simple calculations. They cannot be read off a set of spreadsheets. They are not the product of algorithms. Ratings are predictions about the future. If that does not make them difficult enough, they merge qualitative and quantitative information in the analytical process of their determination. We also know that ratings are very central both to issuers and investors, and this has grown as capital markets have become more important as sources of funding. The consequentiality of rating is a phenomenon of our times.

While the rating process is not ideological in the conscious sense, it clearly does have semantic content, and thus does favor certain

---

67. IOSCO, "Code of Conduct Fundamentals for Credit Rating Agencies," https://www.iosco.org/library/pubdocs/pdf/IOSCOPD482.pdf, accessed July 4, 2020.

68. "WSBI-ESBG Response to BCBS Consultation on Revisions to the Standardised Approach for Credit Risk—Second Consultative Document," March 2016, https://www.wsbi-esbg.org/press/positions/Pages/WSBI-ESBG-response-to-BCBS -consultation-on-revisions-to-the-Standardised-Approach-for-credit-risk -%E2%80%93-second-consultative-doc.aspx, accessed July 4, 2020.

actions and policies by issuers rather than others. There is what I call *the mental framework of rating orthodoxy* at the heart of the rating process.[69] This cognitive frame hinges around the perceived interests of investors, the actors rating agency officials see as their principals. The mental framework of rating orthodoxy, which can be thought of as a feature of the structural power of the agencies, incorporates assumptions about knowledge that defines rating as a technical process, and embraces competition between sources of knowledge. The limitations of this worldview mean that rating is, other things equal, necessarily somewhat pro-cyclical, and therefore likely in times of crisis to potentially make a bad situation worse.

The guiding assumptions of the agencies have shifted over the century or so of their existence from a distinctly diachronic stance at the start of the rating agency industry to one of extreme synchronicity by 2007, at the start of the global financial crisis. As the rating agencies increasingly embraced a synchronic approach to creditworthiness in the years prior to 2007, they seemed to put aside the interests of their self-avowed principals by getting involved in the creation and refinement of new and exotic financial instruments. This transition can be understood through a variety of different approaches, which I discuss in chapter 3.

---

69. Sinclair, *The New Masters of Capital*, 69–70.

3

How to Think about the Agencies

It's the difference between roulette and poker. If
you play roulette and put a million dollars on red, it
doesn't change anything around you. They still spin
the wheel and it doesn't have anything to do with
your bet. But if you play poker and take a card, then
bet a million bucks, every player around you reacts.
They fold, call, or raise and build a strategy based
on your action. A lot of models that look at Bear
[Stearns] treat it like roulette, but it's really poker.
— *Douglas Brunt,* Ghosts of Manhattan

The Enron bankruptcy focused public attention for the first time
on the work of the rating agencies. Until this point, public understanding of the agencies was dominated by the financial press
and business schools. Because of this, the established public view
of the agencies was narrow and did not appreciate the challenges
involved in rating, assuming it to be a simple technical thing, free
of dilemmas, and therefore safe in the hands of the rating agencies.

Thinking about the agencies by scholars has developed, invigo-
rated by the global financial crisis, to the point where it is possible to
identify the emergence of distinct schools of thought. Views will differ on how these ways of thinking can be grouped and differentiated

one from another. I have not given much attention here to views on the rating agencies outside the developed world. My reason for this is that, for the purposes of this book, the agencies that matter are the Big Three and the field of action is the United States and Europe.

After I briefly examine the most important contending approaches to the understanding of rating, I outline what I consider the best way of thinking about the agencies, based on my research and the development of my thinking about these issues. I argue the case that my approach, which I call the social foundations approach to rating, most effectively captures the main characteristics of the agencies, the rating process, and its consequences. In part, my thinking is built on the strengths of the competing schools of thought, although I argue that most thinking about the rating agencies fails to capture the real significance of these organizations. I start with mainstream thinking.

Market-Centered Approaches

What rating agencies do can be thought of as serving a "function" in the economic system.[1] In this view, rating agencies solve a problem in markets that develops when banks no longer sit at the center of the borrowing process. Another way to think about this function is to suggest rating agencies establish psychological "rules of thumb" that make market decisions less costly for participants.[2] As banks have changed their nature, becoming a less significant part

---

1. Scholars in this tradition include Kruck, "Resilient Blunderers" and "Asymmetry in Empowering and Disempowering Private Intermediaries."

2. Jeffrey Heisler, "Recent Research in Behavioral Finance," *Financial Markets, Institutions and Instruments* 3, no. 5 (1994): 78. Also see Judith G. Kelley and Beth A. Simmons, "Politics by Number: Indicators as Social Pressure in International

of the governance of markets, the rating agencies have become more significant. Looking at the process of capital market growth around the world, the developing role of the handful of rating agencies seems strategic in character.

One strand of research focuses on how issuers can obtain better bond ratings.[3] This work has sought to investigate the rating process and work out what produces better outcomes for issuers. This approach assumes that rating agencies are important and that the people in the markets simply must deal with them. Until the mid-1990s, this was the dominant stream of academic research on the rating agencies.

A second tradition has explored what it is that rating agencies bring to the financial markets. Many financial economists tend to be skeptical about the rating agencies. The question for these scholars is whether the agencies provide new information, thus justifying their existence, or are merely pocketing fees from what is a useless service that people in the market are, for some reason, prepared to buy.[4] Skepticism about the agencies and whether they provide useful information means that for some scholars the agencies are best understood as rent-seekers.

A third strand within the market-centered approach to the agencies focuses on the role of the state and law. In this account, whatever power the agencies have in the capital markets is a reflection of delegation from government.[5] Because governments, especially

---

Relations," *American Journal of Political Science* 59, no. 1 (January 2015): 55–70, quote from 57.

3. See, for example, Langohr and Langohr, *The Rating Agencies and Their Credit Ratings*, chap. 4 and the list of references that begins on page 475.

4. Doron Kliger and Oded Sarig, "The Information Value of Bond Ratings," *Journal of Finance* 55, no. 6 (December 2000): 2879–2902.

5. Partnoy, "The Siskel and Ebert of Financial Markets?"

Washington, have used ratings as a way of promoting prudential requirements for pension funds, and have designated specific agencies as suitable for this purpose, these authors see the power of the agencies as simply a reflection of the power of government, not what the agencies have to offer themselves. Scholars in this tradition, sometimes dubbed the regulatory license approach, claim that regulatory changes over the years, especially the advent of NRSRO status, have created a protected niche within which the agencies have been able to institutionalize themselves as a core feature of the architecture of financial markets. This approach argues that attempts to shape financial markets via regulation have backfired and created institutions that exploit their state-protected position, become gatekeepers, and take advantage of other market participants via high fees and poor service.

A variation on this approach, legal license, focuses on the role of US courts in using ratings as "norms of prudence" within the financial community.[6] It assumes an extrinsic explanation for rating being central to the securities markets and ignores possible intrinsic or internal reasons, such as the epistemic authority of the agencies acquired over a long history of rating. Although their agenda appears to be to demonstrate the perversity of the role of government in creating a rating oligopoly, this account does demonstrate that, prima facie, when thinking about the agencies, analysts must consider the role of public power. This is still a market-centered approach because it sees interventions as perverse, messing up the normal or natural functioning of markets.

---

6. Marc Flandreau and Joanna Kinga Sławatyniec, "Understanding Rating Addiction: US Courts and the Origins of Rating Agencies' Regulatory License (1900–1940)," *Financial History Review* 20, no. 3 (2013): 237–257.

Assumptions about information are central to market-centered approaches. The skepticism of financial economists about the probability of the rating agencies providing new or otherwise publicly inaccessible information suggests that information about markets and market participants can be obtained cheaply and easily by observers. It also suggests that market-centric observers do not place a lot of value on the judgments of the agencies, and do not weigh their century-long experience of rating analysis as offering any substantial value to the rating process. This negation of experience and long-run observation suggests a strongly synchronic mindset about markets and institutions such as the agencies. In this worldview, only transparent and measurable information has value.

Given this, when business school analysts do take the agencies seriously it is typically as an unfortunate fact of life that—although seemingly irrational—nevertheless can have a serious impact on the cost of and access to financing.[7] Looked at in this way, the agencies emerge as part of the institutional system that emerged last century to tame markets especially when in crisis, rather than as necessary agents of collective action that make markets work. In this sense, these scholars see the agencies as a nuisance rather than as an aid to efficiency.

The market-centered school makes some positive contributions to the understanding of the rating agencies. The focus on the performance of the agencies is the most tangible dimension of this work. These scholars want to measure the degree to which the agencies matter, and in what circumstances. Market-centered approaches to the agencies are problem-solving in purpose and can be useful to

---

7. A good example of this tradition is the work of Lawrence J. White. See his "The Credit Rating Agencies." Others with related thinking include Soudis, "Credit Rating Agencies and the IPE."

those pursuing specific ratings for their securities issues. The practical engagement of these scholars in trying to produce a better rating system is positive, even if it may be doomed to failure.

Although the market-centered approach to the agencies is pragmatic and can be useful, it is premised on utopian notions about markets and how they work. Implicit here is the idea that markets are spontaneous and natural, rather than social and historical forms of collective human interaction, created, supported, and governed by state and law. This natural conception of markets tends to underestimate the necessity of institutions in solving market problems. Because these approaches do not grant the agencies epistemic authority, they find it hard to fathom the continued existence of the agencies in the wake of the opprobrium directed at the agencies with the onset of the global financial crisis that started in 2007. They cannot solve the major puzzles of this book.

Populist Views

There is a large volume of popular commentary every day on the rating agencies in newspapers and online sources, especially when a rating downgrade is threatened. Much of this commentary is hostile to the agencies, which is sometimes true of scholarly and professional views too.[8] Although it might be tempting to dismiss populist ideas as not very serious, they matter because, cogent or not, collectively held ideas are often consequential in business and politics. Hostility to Wall Street has a long history in American politics and

---

8. An example in this tradition is Klaus C. Engelen, "Das Empire Strikes Back: German Banks Have Had Enough of Standard and Poor's and Other Agencies, and They're Not Going to Take It Anymore," *International Economy* (Winter 2004): 64–71.

has motivated political change since at least the western expansion of the United States after the Civil War.

In addition to the US discussion, there is also much discussion of the agencies and what they do in Europe and in Asia. Much of the professional discussion in Europe, especially associated with the City of London, shares views with the market-centered school. But on the Continent voices are raised in criticism of the US agencies regularly, typically emphasizing their US base and mentality, and the different ways of thinking in Europe. The European sovereign debt crisis that followed the global financial crisis magnified this criticism. These tensions have led to repeated talk about launching European-based rating agencies in the past two decades. Berlin-based Scope was a result of these tensions, established in 2002.[9] Headed by a former S&P executive, Scope uses only publicly available information to produce ratings. Two decades later, despite its ambitions to compete with the Big Three, Scope Ratings remains a very small participant in the global ratings market with just 0.5 percent of the European ratings market.[10] It finances itself, like the Big Three, by charging issuers fees for ratings. In Russia and in emerging markets in Asia the hostility is much greater, perhaps magnified by geopolitical conflicts with the United States.[11] Despite

9. Chris Flood, "Big US Rating Agencies Get New European Rival," *Financial Times*, August 31, 2014, https://www.ft.com/content/3ae000a2-2f5a-11e4-a79c-00144feabdc0, accessed August 21, 2017; Marc Jones, "German Ratings Firm Scope Seeks ECB Recognition," Reuters, August 24, 2016, http://www.reuters.com/article/us-eurozone-ratings-ecb-idUSKCN10Z1EC, accessed August 21, 2017.

10. Olaf Storbeck, "Scope Faces Uphill Struggle to Crack Credit Rating Market," *Financial Times*, January 2, 2020, https://www.ft.com/content/929f5e8c-2bad-11ea-a126-99756bd8f45e, accessed September 12, 2020.

11. "Russia Is So Fed-Up with Western Credit Rating Agencies, It Has Launched Its Own," *The Telegraph*, December 11, 2015, http://www.telegraph.co.uk/finance/economics/12046291/Russia-is-so-fed-up-with-Western-credit-rating-agencies

similar tensions, in 2020 China started to ease restrictions on foreign rating agencies covering Chinese firms.[12]

A key assumption within this way of thinking about the agencies (and finance and banking generally) is the idea that markets are consciously manipulated, and that this produces bad outcomes. The agencies seem to be part of this rigging of the market against what would otherwise be fairer, more "natural" outcomes.

Populist thinking about finance and the rating agencies reflects the reality that business cultures are not universal. This is true within the United States in terms of the gap between big business and other businesses, and it is especially true for the non-US participants in this school of thought, who reject US norms, such as those about law.

The populist perspective on the agencies is useful in that it introduces politics into our understanding of rating. This is in strong contrast to the market-centered school for whom politics is always extrinsic to markets. Even if the populists do not have a well-developed

---

-it-has-launched-its-own.html, accessed August 21, 2017; "Dagong Chief Says Credit Ratings Need 'Chinese Wisdom,'" *Malay Mail Online*, March 26, 2014, http://www.themalaymailonline.com/money/article/dagong-chief-says-credit -ratings-need-chinese-wisdom#TM5MLrhphke1MarZ.97, accessed August 21, 2017. Discussions among the BRICS countries (Brazil, Russia, India, China, and South Africa) about setting up a BRICS rating agency have not been conclusive. Misheck Mutize and Sean Gossel, "BRICS Wants to Set Up an Alternative Rating Agency. Why It May Not Work," *The Conversation*, February 7, 2017, https:// theconversation.com/brics-wants-to-set-up-an-alternative-rating-agency-why-it -may-not-work-72382, accessed August 21, 2017.

12. "Present Tense, Future Market: Financial Coupling in China," *The Economist*, September 5, 2020, 61. I also discussed these issues with Ian Linnell, president of Fitch Ratings, who saw this development as a substantial change in the situation in China and a significant opportunity for the major agencies like his. He noted that this development seems to have stemmed from US-China negotiations undertaken at the very start of the Trump administration. Interview at Canary Wharf, London, September 22, 2020.

understanding of the politics of the rating agencies, they do avoid the utopianism of many of the market-based analysts.

Another useful contribution of this approach is the way it highlights US assumptions implicit in the work of the agencies. Although populism does not have a well-developed understanding of this bias, populists are right in asserting the influence of US origins on what the agencies do. That influence is subtle, but it is woven into the mental framework that lies at the heart of rating.

Populism has also helped expose the distributional implications of Wall Street. This is useful because it helps to shine a light on the broader social and economic implications of the agencies and how they work, potentially suggesting different criteria for an evaluation of the agencies.

Critical Perspectives

Critical thinkers put the rating agencies in context of the capitalist system. Capitalism is a mode of production with implications for social relations and how society is governed. Traditionally, in Marx's schema, people are classified in terms of their relationship to production—whether they own or control production, or simply labor at the means of production owned and controlled by others. Contemporary critical thinkers such as Robert W. Cox understand the agencies as part of the structural power of capital, which they believe has grown in recent decades.[13] This form of power suggests that governments are dependent on private corporations to create employment and tax revenues. In the context of stagnant productivity growth since the 1970s, rising inflation, and

---

13. Robert W. Cox, "Global Perestroika," in Robert W. Cox with Timothy J. Sinclair, *Approaches to World Order* (Cambridge: Cambridge University Press, 1996).

debt problems for states, structural power emboldened institutions of review and discipline like the rating agencies, who were less important when times were good. As debt finance has grown in importance, governments and corporations have sought to develop good relationships with the agencies.[14]

Cox illustrates the role of the agencies in these circumstances by referring to the ratings of the Quebec (1976) and Ontario (1990) provincial governments, and by discussing the case of General Motors in 1991.[15] GM, a "flagship of the US economy," was suddenly revealed to be a "tributary to the financial manipulators of Wall Street" when it was downgraded, suggests Cox. Cox sees the rating agencies as part of this manipulation, "decoupled from production to become an independent power, an autocrat over the real economy."[16]

Cox says the manipulators are driven by short-term synchronic concerns of immediate gain. They are not interested in long-term industrial development, which requires a diachronic mentality. The agencies are, he suggests, part of the rise of what Susan Strange termed "casino capitalism" with its concomitant destruction of jobs and productive capital.[17]

A key assumption of the critical approach is that the capitalist system, or the currently hegemonic variant of capitalism, is in acute crisis. This crisis of weak productivity growth, stagnant incomes, and widening inequalities makes management of capitalism and society increasingly challenging. This poses major problems for governments, which find it hard to raise the resources they need. So, the context in which the rating agencies operate is increasingly a fraught one. Although this increases the power of the agencies, it

---

14. Cox, 298.
15. Cox, 299–300.
16. Cox, 300.
17. Cox, 300.

also means there are likely to be more frequent challenges to the agencies as what they do becomes politicized.

It might seem obvious, but in the critical approach institutions like the rating agencies are not in any sense neutral judges. They are part of capitalism and serve to maintain the social and political relations of capitalism, such as private property. This means the agencies support a specific hegemony of social forces in society through the work they do. Government has only limited independence from capitalism in this account. The state is not a neutral institution. It is a capitalist state, and it has been constrained in recent years by the crisis of capitalism and its own fiscal crisis. In some circumstances the agencies can have significant leverage over states. But this is not always the case, and the circumstances are crucial.

Locating the agencies in a specific social and economic system improves our understanding of what it is the agencies do and why they do it. The crisis-ridden character of the system helps explain the increased power and visibility of the agencies in the past three decades.

The risk with the critical approach to rating agencies is not taking the agencies and what they do seriously enough. If they are just another institution of capitalism, which critical scholars understand as a historical system or structure, why bother studying the agencies themselves? This would be a great shame because our understanding of finance and its relationship to capitalism and the state is not very well developed. How the agencies fit into this, and how what they do changes with circumstances, cannot simply be read off their standing as capitalist institutions. We need to investigate and understand this in concrete terms.[18]

---

18. Other scholars, such as Helleiner and Wang, "Limits to the BRICS' Challenge," and Pagliari, "Who Governs Finance?," take a power-based approach that shares much with Cox, but do not share his systematic anticapitalist stance.

The Social Foundations Approach

Let me explain how best to understand the rating agencies and what they do. This approach is the best route to solving the puzzles I isolated in chapter 1. I call this the social foundations approach, which is derived from critical perspectives, with insights from market-centered thinking.[19] Figure 1 distinguishes different ways of thinking about the agencies based on whether they focus more on structure versus agency on the vertical axis, and whether they focus more on material (brute) or idealist (social) causation on the horizontal axis.[20]

I think purely material explanations for the existence of rating agencies are deceptive. Attempts to verify (or refute) the idea that rating agencies must exist because they serve a purpose have proven inconclusive. Rating agencies must be considered important actors because people view them as important, acting on that understanding in markets. Investors often mimic other investors, "ignoring substantive private information."[21] The fact that people may collectively

---

19. Scholars whose work overlaps with this approach include Carruthers, "From Uncertainty toward Risk"; Paudyn, *Credit Ratings and Sovereign Debt*; Abdelal and Blyth, "Just Who Put You in Charge?"; Nölke, "Financialisation as the Core Problem for a 'Social Europe'"; Natalia Besedovsky, "Financialization as Calculative Practice: The Rise of Structured Finance and the Cultural and Calculative Transformation of Credit Rating Agencies," *Socio-Economic Review* 16, no. 1 (2018): 75; Bart Stellinga, "Why Performativity Limits Credit Rating Reform," *Finance and Society* 5, no. 1 (2019): 20–41; Giulia Mennillo, *Credit Rating Agencies* (Newcastle, UK: Agenda, 2021).

20. I have previously referred to the social foundations approach as the "social facts perspective" in work coauthored with Jeffrey M. Chwieroth. See Jeffrey M. Chwieroth and Timothy J. Sinclair, "How You Stand Depends on How We See: International Capital Mobility as Social Fact," *Review of International Political Economy* 20, no. 3 (2013): 459.

21. David S. Scharfstein and Jeremy C. Stein, "Herd Behavior and Investment," *American Economic Review* 80, no. 3 (June 1990): 465.

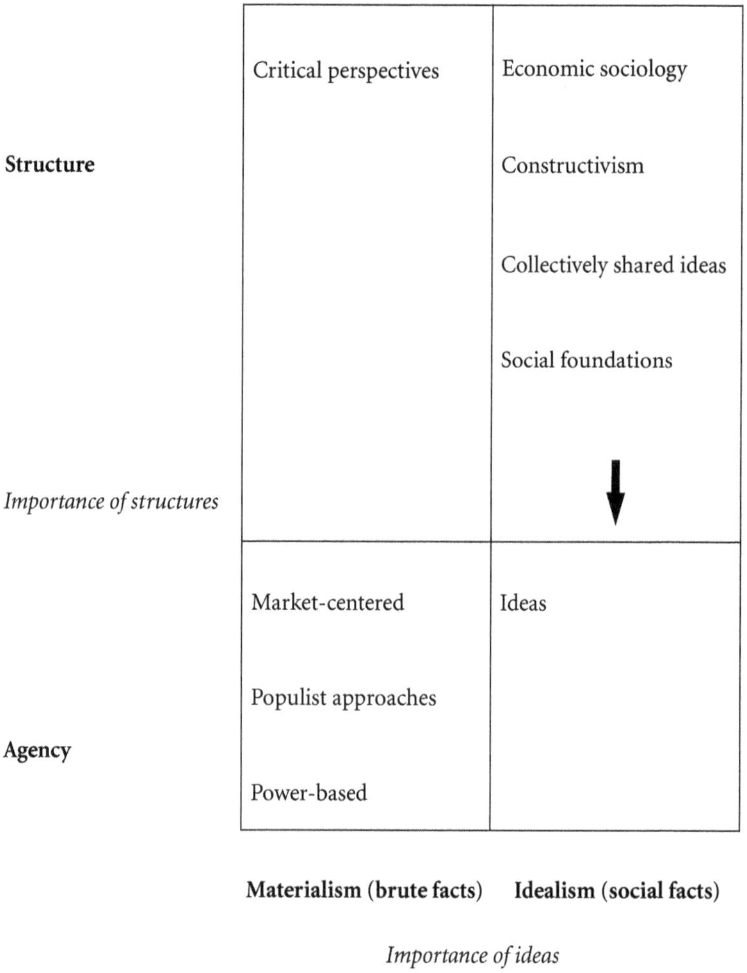

FIGURE 1
Approaches to thinking about the rating agencies. *Source*: Adapted from Chwieroth and Sinclair, "How You Stand Depends on How We See," 461.

view rating agencies as important—irrespective of what purpose the agencies are thought to serve in the scholarly literature—means that markets and debt issuers have strong incentives to act as if participants in the markets take the rating agencies seriously.

In the social foundations view, the significance of rating cannot be reduced, like a mountain or national population, to a "brute" fact that is true (or not) irrespective of shared beliefs about its existence, nor is the meaning of rating determined by the "subjective" facts of individual perception.[22] What is central to the status and consequentiality of rating agencies is what people believe about the agencies, and then act on collectively—even if those beliefs are not true. Indeed, the beliefs may be quite strange to the observer, but if people use them as a guide to action (or inaction) they are significant. Dismissing collective beliefs misses the fact that actors must take account of the existence of social facts in considering their own action. Reflection about the nature and direction of social facts, about what others think and can be expected to do, is characteristic of financial markets.

This approach to understanding the agencies suggests that the source of their power is not just their immediate coercive effect on the cost of borrowing, but their broader impact on ideas and on confidence in markets, institutions, and governments. Because this approach thinks brute *as well as* social facts are important to explanation, because it, like my earlier work on international capital mobility with Chwieroth, seeks to capture the "central role agency has in ideational life," it cannot be reduced to constructivism, even though it is related to constructivism and to economic sociology.[23] The social

---

22. John Gerard Ruggie, *Constructing the World Polity: Essays on International Institutionalization* (New York: Routledge, 1998), 12–13.

23. Chwieroth and Sinclair, "How You Stand Depends on How We See," 466.

foundations approach allows for the social facts status of the Big Three and the ideational contestation seen in the world of rating.[24] Unlike market-centered analysts on the left side of the figure and constructivists (and economic sociologists) on the right, "a more agent-centered approach enables a sharper focus on the persuasive and expressive practices" rating agencies deploy, and this implies a downward arrow to indicate the approach "bleeding into" the bottom-right quadrant.[25] The social foundations approach to rating does a better job of dealing with rating agency power than power-based approaches that focus on simple behavioral notions of "power over." The social foundations approach incorporates the social relations of constitution into structural power, as opposed to just the interaction of particular actors. For example, think of the relations between creditors and debtors—they cannot exist without each other, but have unequal social privileges and differing understandings of who they are, which may serve to obscure the hegemony of groups that have structural power.[26] Sil and Katzenstein have suggested that the approach I take to the agencies can be understood as representative of a tradition they call "analytic eclecticism."[27]

Most ways of thinking about the rating agencies understand them to be external to finance, which is understood as a natural phenomenon, subject to periodic crises because of external interventions. The social foundations view of the agencies recognizes that the agencies are not financial institutions in the narrow sense. They are professional services firms. However, they are bound into the institutions and processes through which finance works. In this sense rating agencies are endogenous to finance (and thus to financial cri-

---

24. Chwieroth and Sinclair, 467.
25. Chwieroth and Sinclair, 467.
26. Chwieroth and Sinclair, 468.
27. Sil and Katzenstein discuss my approach in *Beyond Paradigms*, 118–125.

ses) rather than being external or exogenous. Scholars with exogenous assumptions share the views of Friedrich von Hayek and Milton Friedman. Their views are associated with attacks on the mixed economy model of state intervention popular in much of the developed world after the Great Depression of the 1930s. These thinkers took it as axiomatic that markets, when left to their own devices, are efficient allocators of resources. For them, financial crisis is a deviation from the normal state of the market.

Eugene Fama's Efficient Markets Hypothesis (EMH) in its strong form has come to represent this tradition of thought.[28] The basic idea of the EMH is that because prices for stocks, bonds, derivatives, and so on are always based on all the available information, they must reflect the fundamental value of these securities. Real-world markets are efficient in that securities trade at equilibrium between supply and demand. No price gouging is possible if the EMH holds true. In the strong form EMH is a remarkable claim about information and how it is incorporated into market prices.

Given that exogenous thinkers assume markets work efficiently, this tradition focuses on "external" causes, especially government failure, as the cause of crisis. Friedman, for example, blamed the Great Depression of the 1930s on what he considered to be incorrect Federal Reserve policy in 1929 and 1930, rather than the effects of the stock market crash in October 1929.[29]

The endogenous account, by contrast, says finance has its own characteristics that drive it internally. For Marx and Polanyi, finance is driven by the internal "laws of motion" of the capitalist mode of production. These produce constant change and upheaval, not

---

28. Eugene F. Fama and Merton H. Miller, *The Theory of Finance* (New York: Holt, Rinehart and Winston, 1972).

29. Charles P. Kindleberger and Robert Z. Aliber, *Manias, Panics and Crashes: A History of Financial Crises*, 5th ed. (New York: Palgrave Macmillan, 2005), 72.

equilibrium between demand and supply. For Keynes, the "animal spirits" or passions of speculation give rise to playing with chance.[30] Typical of the endogenous perspective is Keynes's idea that market traders do not merely integrate information coming from outside the markets in the wider, real economy, but are focused on what other traders are doing, in an effort to anticipate their buy/sell activities, and thus make money from them (or at least avoid losing more money than the market average). As Abdelal and Blyth have argued, even if ratings are out of date by the time they are issued, made inaccurate by complex and lightning-fast trading in global markets, ratings generate prices that make it possible to construct portfolios.[31] Without rating "such prices and estimates of risk[,] complex markets cannot function."[32] Katzenstein and Stephen Nelson agree, claiming that it is in the participants' and regulators' interest that the "veil of highly technical analysis" around rating be maintained.[33] Abdelal and Blyth go on to suggest that the agencies have reached what Keynes might have called the *fourth degree*: "Market sentiments, and therefore the viability of the sovereigns' policy stances, are shaped and affected by the ratings, which are themselves demanded by the agents affected by the ratings."[34]

---

30. As noted earlier, Keynes suggested that the essence of finance is not, as most supposed, a matter of picking the best stocks, based on an economic analysis of which should rise in value in future. Anticipating what other traders in the market were likely to do was more relevant. John Maynard Keynes, *The General Theory of Employment, Interest and Money* (Amherst, NY: Prometheus, 1997 [1936]), 156. See also George A. Akerlof and Robert J. Shiller, *Animal Spirits: How Human Psychology Drives the Economy and Why It Matters for Global Capitalism* (Princeton, NJ: Princeton University Press, 2009), 133.

31. Abdelal and Blyth, "Just Who Put You in Charge?," 56.

32. Abdelal and Blyth, 57.

33. Peter J. Katzenstein and Stephen C. Nelson, "Reading the Right Signals and Reading the Signals Right: IPE and the Financial Crisis of 2008," *Review of International Political Economy* 20, no. 5 (2013): 1117.

34. Abdelal and Blyth, "Just Who Put You in Charge?," 57.

Given this, rumors, norms and other features of social life are part of a well-developed understanding of how finance works.[35] On this account, finance is subject to the pathologies of social life, like any other activity in which humans engage. This is an image of finance far from the self-regulating conception that characterizes the EMH. The "animal spirits" identified by Keynes and elaborated on by George Akerlof and Robert Shiller do not produce stability in the market for assets as they do in the market for goods. In the absence of equilibrium, there is no limit to the expansion of market enthusiasm for financial assets or houses, producing what we have come to call a "bubble" economy. Unfortunately, as we know, bubbles tend to deflate in an unpredictable manner, with typically negative consequences.

The impulse when there is a crisis involving the agencies is to regulate them by creating a framework of rules that are "heavier" or "harder" or somehow more "serious." The prevailing understanding seems to be that the people involved were doing things wrong. It is as if the mechanic fixing your car has fitted the wrong parts. But the machine analogy will not do for global finance. Finance is not a physical phenomenon. While financial markets may display regularities in normal times, these regularities are not lawlike. Change is an ever-present feature of all social mechanisms, including finance.

John Searle made a useful distinction between regulative rules that "regulate antecedently or independently existing forms of behavior" and more architectural forms of rule. The latter, or "constitutive rules, do not merely regulate, they create or define new

---

35. A recent study in the behavioral finance tradition is focused on addressing the role of beliefs "because changes in expectations can trigger massive dislocations" such as after the Lehman bankruptcy. See Nicola Gennaioli and Andrei Shleiffer, *A Crisis of Beliefs: Investor Psychology and Financial Fragility* (Princeton, NJ: Princeton University Press, 2018), 5.

forms of behavior."[36] He goes on to suggest that chess and football are only possible by following their rules. The rules are constitutive or architectural. They make the game. The point here is that public and elite panic during the global financial crisis focused on regulative rules (or the lack of them) and those who allegedly broke them. But this is not the problem with rating agencies, or what brought about the global financial crisis. The deep, constitutive rules that constitute the markets were damaged by the panic. Behavior that is guided by constitutive rules is hard to put back together again once those rules are broken.

The social foundations perspective suggests that finance is not now and never was a smoothly functioning, machinelike system despite the plethora of calculative techniques deployed in the financial markets.[37] Given this, we should expect turbulence and change, euphoria and dysphoria in the markets, although these expectations run counter to conventional assumptions about markets. These diachronic characteristics of finance are normal and are challenging for institutions like rating agencies to fully anticipate effectively, even though the agencies have always sought to incorporate business and industrial cycles into their analysis. These assumptions suggest that in times of change, when there is much financial innovation, the choices made by the agencies are always likely to be difficult. They will get them wrong.

A key feature of the social foundations perspective on rating is that it focuses on collectively held ideas about institutions because

36. John R. Searle, *Speech Acts: An Essay in the Philosophy of Language* (Cambridge: Cambridge University Press, 1969), 33.

37. For evidence of the limits of formalization, see Akos Rona-Tas and Stefanie Hiss, "The Role of Ratings in the Subprime Mortgage Crisis: The Art of Corporate and the Science of Consumer Credit Rating," in *Markets on Trial: The Economic Sociology of the US Financial Crisis*, ed. Michael Lounsbury and Paul M. Hirsch (Bingley, UK: Emerald House, 2010), 113–153.

collective understandings, or what Abdelal and Blyth call "conventional judgment," make institutions consequential (or not).[38] How those collective ideas came about, and how they may change, are important research questions. This puts the focus not so much on what agencies do, but rather on what people observe and collectively agree they are doing. This means that research on rating agencies is relational. To be robust, it must deal with the agencies in their social context. Rating agencies are not like components we can just clip into a machine. This is why, when considering the role of the agencies in the global financial crisis, we have to take seriously the rhetoric about what it was the agencies were supposed to have done even when we can show it to be unfounded. In analysis, it is crucial to distinguish this from what actually happened, in order to generate the most convincing understanding.

Authority is an important characteristic of the relationship between the agencies and context.[39] By authority, I mean the epistemic qualities of the agencies, as perceived by their audience, the acknowledgment that, like judges in the courts, the rating agencies are effective, experienced, and wise judges of creditworthiness. Central to this process is deferral. Accepting the judgments of the agencies because of their eminence means that people in the markets, in politics, and in the wider public surrender their judgment to the agencies. David Lake has noted that the agencies "enforce their authority" by refusing to rate some debt securities and, of

---

38. Abdelal and Blyth, "Just Who Put You in Charge?," 53–54. On the role of social conventions in financial markets, also see Stephen C. Nelson and Peter J. Katzenstein, "Uncertainty, Risk, and the Financial Crisis of 2008," *International Organization* 68, no. 2 (2014): 361–392.

39. Malcolm Campbell-Verduyn, *Professional Authority after the Global Financial Crisis* (London: Palgrave, 2017), 34–35.

course, by the threat of downgrading their ratings.[40] The robustness of the agencies' authority and its resilience in the face of alleged mistakes or "rating failures" is a significant characteristic of the agencies, typically frustrating to nonsocial approaches to the agencies. Focusing on authority explains why we have a rating Big Three that excludes all the other rating agencies, even those who are NRSROs, none of which have significant epistemic assets.

RATING AGENCIES ARE intriguing institutions. People in the rich world only realized they were important starting in the early 1990s, as countries like New Zealand and Canada began to experience serious fiscal problems. Before this time, the agencies were only of interest to investment professionals. This means that serious social science efforts to comprehend the agencies are less than thirty years old or so. It took some years for diverging schools of thought to appear, but now the shape of a market and a critical school seems clear. More protean is the populist perspective on the agencies, which has been less developed by scholars than by popular media. All three schools of thought have their uses and inform the social foundations approach I discussed at greater length in this chapter. Each of the first three suffers from myopia, and all seem to allow their view of how they want the agencies to be to get in the way of their understanding of what it is the agencies are, what they do, and why it matters. In this sense, the social foundations approach I presented in this chapter is the most realistic approach, and most useful for an effective understanding of how the agencies fell into crisis and then rose again, as I investigate in the following chapters.

---

40. David A. Lake, "Rightful Rules: Authority, Order, and the Foundations of Global Governance," *International Studies Quarterly* 54 (2010): 587–613, quote from 606.

4

The Agencies and Financial Innovation

> When the music stops . . . things will be compli-
> cated. But as long as the music is playing, you've got
> to get up and dance. We're still dancing.
> —*Chuck Prince, CEO Citigroup*, Financial Times,
> *July 9, 2007*

Things did become "complicated" and on a massive, unprecedented scale in the eighteen months after Prince uttered these
words. The dancing stopped dead, replaced by a breakdown of trust
among traditional market players and a rush for the exit. Citigroup
eventually received $476.2 billion in cash and guarantees, the most
of any bank bailed out by the US government.[1] This chapter is
concerned with the dancing, how the dancing came to an abrupt
halt, and the role of the rating agencies in it all.

At their establishment in the early decades of the twentieth
century the agencies were a constraining force on finance. This is
not surprising given that the agencies were founded in the wake of
the 1907 crash and came to maturity during the Great Depression

---

1. Nitasha Tiku, "Citigroup Received More Bailout Money Than Any Other
Bank," *New York*, March 16, 2011, http://nymag.com/intelligencer/2011/03/citibank
_received_more_bailout.html, accessed August 19, 2019.

of the 1930s. The agencies supported the growth of the industrial mass production system in the decades following World War II, dominated by US corporations such as General Motors and IBM. The conservative, diachronic stance of the agencies fitted with the conservative Wall Street mainstream that resisted the high-yield debt financing of the 1980s, led by investment bankers such as Michael Milken. For Milken, the skeptical stance of the agencies denied growth-focused companies low-cost financing, favoring slower-growing market incumbents. Although Milken went to prison in 1991 and paid a $600 million fine for breaches of the securities laws in the United States, his desire to reform the securities market became mainstream thinking in the 1990s. The provision in the Glass-Steagall (Banking) Act of 1933 that separated banking from investment banking with the intent of insulating savings and payments from volatile securities speculation was abolished by the Gramm-Leach-Bliley Act passed in late 1999, opening the way for banks to engage in lucrative investment banking transactions.

Falling interest rates in the United States following collapse of the tech bubble in 2001 led to a hunt for yield by investors unhappy with the poor returns they could receive from regular investments. This search did not focus on lending to developing countries, as in the 1980s, but on financial innovation on Wall Street and in the City of London. The energies released by the Gramm-Leach-Bliley Act expanded the number of institutions that could focus on trading these high-margin securities in secondary markets. Now the big US banks could participate for the first time, bringing the resources funded by their insured deposit-taking activities and large balance sheets. The new financial instruments that proliferated to meet this demand played a major role in the transformation of the agencies away from their traditional role in American finance.

During the postwar diachronic era of rating conservatism Fitch had been a minor player.[2] The second-rate status of Fitch started to change in 1989 and especially from 1997 when acquisitions and mergers increased the size and coverage of Fitch. This is important because regulation and market norms typically require ratings by two agencies. With three sizeable and well-known companies competing for market share for the first time, and with Moody's being reestablished as a separate corporate entity in 1998, the rating system moves from a comfortable duopoly in the twentieth century to greater competitiveness in the twenty-first. None of the agencies could assume they would get the available business anymore, as they had for decades prior to the resurgence of Fitch.

Securitization and the Agencies

Starting in 2007, and for years afterward, discussions of what became known as the global financial crisis revolved around new securities referred to collectively as structured finance. Structured finance is not intuitive like a bond or a loan. When a corporation issues a bond, that corporation may go bankrupt if it fails to repay bondholders, who then have recourse to all the assets of the company. This is not how structured finance works, because trusts intermediate the process of raising capital between borrowers and lenders. Lenders do not have recourse to the assets of the company behind the fund, should the fund fail.

On top of this, a whole new world of derivative products developed to insure these trusts, allowing traders to make money by buying and selling these derivatives in secondary markets. Later, when

---

2. Although Fitch was a small company, its long-term credit rating scale was influential, and was licensed by S&P in the 1920s.

the financial crisis was in full swing, the conceptual and substantive challenges of structured finance meant that when bankers, especially senior managers, were asked about these financial instruments they were sometimes unable to give convincing answers about how they worked.[3] Many observers blamed structured finance for the crisis. Given the seeming lack of understanding among senior finance professionals about these instruments, it is no wonder panic developed within the markets as conditions deteriorated.

In what follows, I am going to discuss what structured finance was supposed to achieve, how it worked concretely, how the agencies were involved in making structured finance work, and the revisions to ratings as the crisis got under way in 2007 and 2008. The rating of structured finance is certainly not a good story, but this account is not the story commonly told. Subsequently, I highlight the extreme financial innovation of repurchase agreement ("repos") and their role in transforming local financial distress into the global financial crisis.

Like bonds, structured finance is a promise to repay the lender or investor. The major motivation to raise money by selling structured securities rather than ordinary bonds is to reduce the cost of borrowing to the issuer. Lower costs follow from establishing a pool of diversified assets with "greater cash flow certainty than the credit of a single company."[4] This means the pool will attract stronger credit ratings, allowing issuers to pay less to investors than they

---

3. *The Financial Crisis Inquiry Report* called the lack of understanding by senior management, such as the reported "ignorance of the terms and risks" of AIG's $79 billion derivatives portfolio, "stunning instances of governance breakdowns and irresponsibility" (xix).

4. Sylvain Raynes and Ann Rutledge, *The Analysis of Structured Securities: Precise Risk Measurement and Capital Allocation* (New York: Oxford University Press, 2003), vii.

would otherwise when they sell them structured finance instruments such as collateralized debt obligations (CDOs) and collateralized loan obligations (CLOs).[5] A "structure of protection" is crafted, based on anticipated losses over time, giving different rights to streams of income, based on diverging appetites for risk among investors. Compare this with debt securities from emerging markets where the risk of loss may be uncertain and impossible to calculate.[6] As noted above, in contrast to bonds, structured securities are legally separate from the assets of the companies instigating their creation and sale. This is done by putting the assets beyond the reach of that company, in the hands of a trustee, so that in any future bankruptcy of the originator, creditors will not have access to these assets.[7]

Derivatives based on transactions within the structured finance market were private, unregulated over-the-counter (OTC) contracts not traded on exchanges. Credit counterparties did not know the extent to which their counterparties were exposed to derivative risk. The total notional value of all derivatives of whatever type was $600 trillion in 2007.[8] This seems like a fantastic figure, and it turns out it is. Of this $600 trillion, around $60 trillion was the value of credit default swaps (CDS). The rest were interest rate contracts, foreign exchange contracts, equity-linked contracts, and commodity contracts (for the future prices of pork bellies, soybeans, and similar commodities). CDS is a form of insurance against the default of collateralized debt obligations, widely used to provide

---

5. Implicit here, as Wolf suggests, is the idea that structured finance can make the financial system more resilient. Martin Wolf, *The Shifts and the Shocks* (New York: Penguin, 2015), 119.

6. Raynes and Rutledge, *The Analysis of Structured Securities*, 3.

7. Raynes and Rutledge, 4.

8. Bank of England, *Financial Stability Report*, London, October 2008, 21.

credit protection in the structured finance market, allowing securities to be rated higher than they otherwise would be.[9] The $60 trillion figure exaggerates their real value. When marked to market, the gross market value at current prices was $14.5 trillion at the end of 2007 for all derivatives. A process of bilateral netting further reduces this figure to counterparties to $3.3 trillion. Of this figure, the Bank of England says 65 percent of the exposure of market participants was supported by collateral. So, it turns out that the derivatives market built up around structured finance is much smaller than it seems at first glance when the $600 trillion headline figure is quoted. Most of the $3.3 trillion worth of derivatives were supported by prime assets and collateral. In the primary market, only $0.7 trillion of the $10.7 trillion in residential mortgage-backed securities (RMBS) were subprime.[10]

How Did Securitization Work?

Securitization involved several different institutions buying and selling financial assets from each other, as shown in figure 2. The relationships between these institutions were supported by mutual trust in the probity and creditworthiness of each counterparty and confidence in the market and supporting institutions, such as the law of contract.

The securitization chain began with people borrowing money to buy houses. These mortgages, which might be originated by local banks or by specialist mortgage companies such as Countrywide

---

9. Ben S. Bernanke, *The Federal Reserve and the Financial Crisis* (Princeton, NJ: Princeton University Press, 2013), 49.

10. Bank of England, *Financial Stability Report*, London, October 2007, 20.

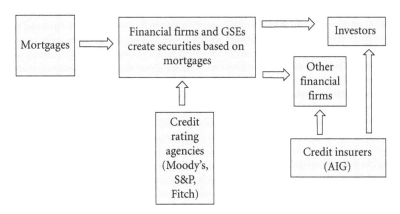

The Securitization Chain. *Source*: Adapted from Bernanke, *The Federal Reserve and the Financial Crisis*, 70.

Financial, were then sold on to large financial firms and the US government-sponsored enterprises (GSEs) Fannie Mae and Freddie Mac, that had a remit to widen access to housing to lower socioeconomic groups.[11] These larger firms pool these different assets and create securities such as collateralized debt obligations. It is in this process of creating these securities that the big firms use the services of the rating agencies. Not all these securities were AAA rated by the agencies. Typically, arranged in a hierarchy as depicted in figure 3, there were different tranches and ratings depending on their legal claims to the cash flow from the mortgages and protection from default provided by insurance.[12] The tranches were likened to the game of Jenga in the movie version of *The Big Short*. In

---

11. Bernanke, *The Federal Reserve and the Financial Crisis*, 65.

12. For the complexities built on top of this basic idea, see Ann Rutledge and Sylvain Raynes, *Elements of Structured Finance* (New York: Oxford University Press, 2010), 129–157. A more accessible account can be found in Matt Taibbi,

the movie, the Jared Vennett character dramatically illustrates how homeowner default causes the Jenga tower to collapse.[13]

What Did the Agencies Do?

As controversy emerged about the rating of structured finance in 2007 and 2008, most observers assumed they understood the role of the agencies in structured finance. They generalized from the process of rating corporate bonds. But this is like assuming you understand how a 2020 Toyota Prius works because you understand how a 1933 Ford V8 functions. There are just enough superficial similarities between the two things to allow for complete misunderstanding.

Creditworthiness is the key issue in both corporate bonds and structured finance. But the focus of rating securitization is no longer on issuers, where the issuer's capacity and willingness to pay is the concern. The assets and the associated flows of cash have been legally separated from issuers, and now belong to a special purpose vehicle (SPV) or trust. This process is called subordination. Structured investment vehicles (SIVs) run by banks buy these products and hold them off–balance sheet.[14] The result of subordination "is

---

Griftopia: A Story of Bankers, Politicians, and the Most Audacious Power Grab in American History (New York: Spiegel and Grau, 2011), 85.

13. The problem with the Jenga analogy is that in the movie, Vennett destroys the tower from the top. But instability typically emerges from the least creditworthy tranches, which one might imagine are at the bottom, where the worst credits reside (as depicted in figure 3). A better analogy might be a Champagne waterfall. Here the wine is poured from the top. The top glasses are filled, just as the AAA tranches at the top fill with money. The bottom glasses (and tranches) get what is left, if anything. The expectation lower-rated tranches would do less well is there in the very conception of securitization (and their ratings).

14. Tracy Alloway, "Search for Yield Boosts Esoteric ABS," *Financial Times*, August 30, 2012, https://www.ft.com/content/a906f80a-f2a9-11e1-ac41-00144feabdc0, accessed October 8, 2018.

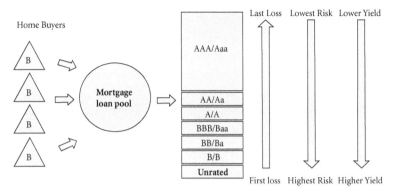

F<small>IGURE</small> 3
Tranches. *Source*: Adapted from Tyler Durden (pseud.), "In Watershed
Event, Europe Plans to Securitize Sovereign Debt," https://www.zerohedge
.com/news/2017-05-30/watershed-event-europe-unveils-plan-securitize
-sovereign-debt, accessed September 18, 2018.

that a collection of loans that in toto would be too risky to be rated
as 'investment grade' now has parts (tranches) that qualify," allowing pension funds, regulated to invest only in investment grade
assets, to buy these products.[15]

Matthew Watson, citing Gillian Tett, suggests that "there is simply no economic reason to assume that a step increase in creditworthiness can be secured merely through the strategic repackaging
of assets."[16] Paul Langley has noted how the purported failures of
specific ratings became a public issue, but has expressed regret that
the contradictions inherent in rating risk itself did not become an

15. Rona-Tas and Hiss, "The Role of Ratings in the Subprime Mortgage Crisis," 126.

16. Matthew Watson, *Uneconomic Economics and the Crisis of the Model World*
(Basingstoke, UK: Palgrave Macmillan, 2014), 30. Tett's book is *Fool's Gold: How
Unrestrained Greed Corrupted a Dream, Shattered Global Markets and Unleashed
a Catastrophe* (New York: Little, Brown, 2009).

issue.[17] Stephen Bell and Andrew Hindmoor argue that the agencies "played a major role in legitimating and popularizing securitization."[18] The quality of structured finance ratings deteriorated in the real estate boom years prior to the onset of the crisis.[19] Nicholas Dunbar notes the deterioration in underlying analytical culture at Moody's.[20] Eric Posner characterizes this as the consequence of a "race to the bottom" between competing rating agencies.[21] Robert Shiller suggests that the rating agencies had become like so many "lenient teachers who gave out too many As."[22] Donald MacKenzie has suggested the key problem with these ratings is they lost sight of the risks of the underlying assets.[23] Rather than taking the credit analysis all the way back to the quality of the mortgages themselves and undertaking a bottom-up analysis, these ratings treated CDOs as discrete entities and treated their ratings as if they were corporate bonds. This approach neglected the issue of correlation, underestimating the likelihood that different financial instruments would deteriorate in value at the same time. Recent work by Juan Ospina and Harald Uhlig challenges this view, suggesting

17. Paul Langley, *The Everyday Life of Global Finance: Saving and Borrowing in Anglo-America* (Oxford: Oxford University Press, 2008), 237.

18. Stephen Bell and Andrew Hindmoor, *Masters of the Universe, Slaves of the Market* (Cambridge, MA: Harvard University Press, 2015), 189.

19. Adam Ashcraft, Paul Goldsmith-Pinkham, and James Vickery, "MBS Ratings and the Mortgage Credit Boom" *Federal Reserve Bank of New York Staff Reports*, No. 449, May 2010, 4.

20. Nicholas Dunbar, *The Devil's Derivatives* (Boston: Harvard Business Review Press, 2011), 65–68.

21. Eric A. Posner, *Last Resort: The Financial Crisis and the Future of Bailouts* (Chicago: University of Chicago Press, 2018), 31.

22. Robert J. Shiller, *Finance and the Good Society* (Princeton, NJ: Princeton University Press, 2012), 52.

23. Donald MacKenzie, "Unlocking the Language of Structured Securities," *Financial Times*, August 19, 2010, https://www.ft.com/content/8127989a-aae3-11df-9e6b-00144feabdc0, accessed September 18, 2012.

that improper ratings of RMBS were not a major factor in the financial crisis of 2008.[24]

According to William Harrington, a former Moody's official, the approach taken by the rating agencies to asset-backed securities failed "to take into account adequate counterparty risk," assuming all involved in the markets shared the same norms and appetite for risk.[25] Jerome Fons, another ex-Moody's staffer, has suggested that the lack of recent experience of widespread decline in home prices, among other issues, undermined the ability of the raters to accurately anticipate the housing asset price downturn.[26] About structured finance, Fons suggests:

---

24. Juan Ospina and Harald Uhlig, "Mortgage-Backed Securities and the Financial Crisis of 2008: A Post Mortem," NBER Working Paper 24509 (Cambridge, MA: National Bureau of Economic Research, April 2018).

25. William Harrington, paraphrased in Madison Marriage, "Ex-Moody's Staff Raise Alarm over ABS 'Meltdown': Asset-Backed Securities Rated Too High," *Financial Times*, November 10, 2013, https://www.ft.com/content/6b8cfc2c-4861 -11e3-a3ef-00144feabdc0#axzz2kZHQUysc, accessed October 8, 2018. Harington has made multiple contributions to the debate on the problems with the agencies. Most significant is his "Comment on SEC Proposed Rules for Nationally Recognized Statistical Rating Organizations," file number S7-18-11, August 8, 2011, https://www.sec.gov/comments/s7-18-11/s71811-33.pdf, accessed October 22, 2018. This is discussed in Henry Blodget, "Moody's Analyst Breaks Silence: Says Rating Agency Rotten to Core with Conflicts," *Business Insider*, August 19, 2011, https://www.businessinsider.com/moodys-analyst-conflicts-corruption-and-greed -2011-8?IR=T, accessed October 22, 2018. On Harrington, see Joris Luyendijk, *Swimming with Sharks: My Journey into the World of the Bankers* (London: Guardian Books, 2015), 156–160.

26. Jerome S. Fons, "White Paper on Rating Competition and Structured Finance," January 10, 2008, included in "Credit Rating Agencies and the Financial Crisis," 80, www.gpo.gov/fdsys/pkg/CHRG-110hhrg51103/pdf/CHRG-110hhrg51103 .pdf, accessed December 11, 2018. This is a point also made by Bruce G. Carruthers, "Knowledge and Liquidity: Institutional and Cognitive Foundations of the Subprime Crisis," in *Markets on Trial: The Economic Sociology of the US Financial Crisis*, ed. Michael Lounsbury and Paul M. Hirsch (Bingley, UK: Emerald House, 2010), 164. Carruthers lists other mistakes made by the agencies, including divergence from their

The role of rating agencies is particularly important to the structured finance process. Investors rely on agency ratings when making purchase decisions because of the opacity. . . . Moreover, the tools to analyze credit risk, even with transparent assets, are beyond the grasp of many investors. Rating methods are quite technical, often relying on advanced statistical techniques. Documentation supporting a transaction can be equally daunting, reading more like a legal brief than helpful financial guidance. . . . A solid understanding of how to value structured securities remains elusive. No one "model" dominates pricing practices in structured finance.[27]

He goes on to suggest that the business of rating structured securities is highly competitive. The fees tend to be higher, he suggests, and notes that structured finance was probably the most important product line for the agencies prior to the financial crisis, making up about 40 percent of their income. The rapid growth of this business in the years prior to the crisis pushed up the price/earnings ratios of rating agency shares, generating "intense pressure for each agency to see its structured finance practice thrive."[28] This led, suggested Fons, to widespread "rating shopping" by issuers. In this phenomenon, "reputation risk is in effect traded for short-term gain" by the rating agencies. Bankers were able to "wield tremendous power and play the rating agencies off of one another." This led to pressure on protection or support levels for structured finance, so that these descended to the "lowest possible val-

internal procedures and models. See Carruthers, "Knowledge and Liquidity," 164–165. Shiller discusses the expectations of the rating agencies about the direction of the housing market in Robert J. Shiller, *The Subprime Solution: How Today's Global Financial Crisis Happened and What to Do about It* (Princeton, NJ: Princeton University Press, 2008), 50–51.

27. Fons, "White Paper," 80.
28. Fons, 80.

ues as agencies maneuver[ed] to maintain market share."[29] These low support levels could be sustained when house values were rising, but not when they fell and fell hard.

Bruce Carruthers discusses the emergence and spread of financial tools, such as the Gaussian Copula, which were quickly adopted by the agencies, and suggests that

> widespread confidence in the technical methods used by rating agencies to evaluate structured financial products combined with strong social integration among an elite to produce an audience that realized only late in the game that it did not really know what it thought it knew. Because of the "Keynesian beauty contest"–quality of the situation, even those who questioned the ratings put aside such doubts so long as many others continued to rely on the ratings. There was too much money to be made in the meantime.[30]

Alice Bamford and Donald MacKenzie suggest that the Gaussian copula as used by the agencies was subject to gaming by issuers of structured financial products.[31] The challenge for them was to find the highest-yielding package of debt "that would nevertheless produce an instrument that could achieve the high ratings necessary for it to be sold profitably."[32] They argue that although the ratings profiles of structured finance "remained broadly stable through" the period leading up to the global financial crisis, "the quality of the debts that made them up deteriorated."[33] Bamford and MacKenzie note that rating assumptions about the housing market were "perfectly defensible in the light of experience before the bursting

---

29. Fons, 80.

30. Carruthers, "Knowledge and Liquidity," 168.

31. Alice Bamford and Donald MacKenzie, "Counterperformativity," *New Left Review* 113 (September-October 2018): 97–121.

32. Bamford and MacKenzie, 116.

33. Bamford and MacKenzie, 116.

of the price bubble."[34] They argue that these assumptions "made possible, via their gaming by market participants," the creation, in a process they dub counterperformativity, "securities that radically undermined" those assumptions in turn.[35]

Ann Rutledge, another ex-Moody's official, argues (with Robert Litan) that the issue with structured finance ratings revealed by the global financial crisis is an information problem. Credit ratings of structured finance are not about the ability (and willingness) of an entity to repay. Ratings in the structured world, because of the confinement of the debt to a trust or SPV, must, they assert, be about the cash in a dedicated pool belonging to the trust or SPV, which is then distributed to the tranches according to the legal structure of the security, as depicted in figure 3. This "requires," they argue, "numbers, or a cardinal rather than an ordinal (lettered) scale."[36] The ordinal rating scales, which provide a ranking of risk, are depicted in table 1. But ordinal rankings are misleading when it comes to the specific characteristics of structured securities, suggest Rutledge and Litan. The cash flow must be counted, and the best way of representing cash flow in ratings is via cardinal ratings, not a ranking. The lack of an agreed public benchmark for structured ratings is, they suggest, "equivalent to saying no two credit rating agencies count cash the same way."[37] Agreement on standard metrics, or a cardinal rating system, would be difficult for competing rating organizations.

Carruthers has suggested that using the "very same rating categories" in rating structured finance as had been used in rating corporate bonds for many years served to "'domesticate' the exoticism

---

34. Bamford and MacKenzie, 116–117.

35. Bamford and MacKenzie, 117.

36. Ann Rutledge and Robert E. Litan, "A Real Fix for Credit Ratings," *Economic Studies at Brookings*, Brookings Institution, Washington, DC, June 2014, ii.

37. Rutledge and Litan, ii.

and mystery that CDOs would have otherwise possessed," functioning like a "seal of approval."[38] Putting all "financial instruments, regardless of their underlying structure or the nature of the debtor, within a single schema masked important heterogeneity and encouraged investors to treat financial options as equivalent simply because they were put into the same category."[39] This created major problems when Moody's and S&P began to downgrade CDOs in 2007. He suggests that the mental equivalences set up by using the same rating scale "induced a cascade of doubt that spread through the financial markets" at this point, inducing a "general unwillingness" to hold structured finance instruments of any sort about which there was the "brutal force of cascading doubt."[40]

Different sources, including people I interviewed on Wall Street, highlighted the way Moody's pursued the structured finance business in the years leading up to the crisis. One highly credible interview source suggested Moody's actually invented structured finance at the end of the 1970s, an innovation not usually attributed to the agency.[41] Sam Jones, writing in the magazine of the *Financial Times*, focuses on the erosion of the comfortable rating duopoly because of the rise of Fitch, especially the implications for rating shopping.[42] He

---

38. Carruthers, "Knowledge and Liquidity," 162.

39. Carruthers, 174.

40. Carruthers, 171–172.

41. In modern times, that role is usually given to Robert F. Dall and Lewis S. Ranieri. See Landon Thomas Jr., "Robert F. Dall, Mastermind of Mortgage-Backed Bonds, Dies at 81," *New York Times*, November 18, 2015, https://www .nytimes.com/2015/11/19/business/dealbook/robert-f-dall-mastermind-of -mortgage-backed-bonds-dies-at-81.html, accessed October 22, 2018. Historically, as Carruthers shows, farm mortgages were first securitized in the 1870s and 1880s. Carruthers, "Knowledge and Liquidity," 160.

42. Sam Jones, "How Moody's Faltered," *FT Magazine*, October 17, 2008, https://www.ft.com/content/65892340-9b1a-11dd-a653-000077b07658, accessed October 22, 2018.

also focused on the key role attributed to Brian Clarkson. Clarkson, a lawyer, joined Moody's in 1991.[43] By 1997, he was in charge of the structured finance division at the firm. Jones suggests that, in the face of falling market share, Clarkson sought to refocus Moody's analysts on issuers. This shift in who was understood to be the principal and who the agent within Moody's was magnified by the flotation of Moody's as a public company in 2000. Jones quotes Rutledge, who suggests that she and her colleagues "were lily white" in the mid-1990s when she worked for Moody's in structured finance. "But," she notes, "then the centre of gravity in Moody's shifted. Moody's went public." With the shift came a new culture or identity, in which analysts enjoyed corporate hospitality with clients, something unthinkable in the austere Moody's of the past. Jones quotes Rutledge observing that research and development on structured finance slowed down in the late 1990s. She notes that "the banks caught up [with Moody's]. And then they came to be the ones in the lead." Moody's and the other rating firms became "passive participants" in analyzing the facts and probabilities of the deals. The agencies struggled to keep up with what the banks were devising.

When the Agencies Changed Their Minds

Distinct from the contribution the agencies made to the growth of the structured finance market is the impact their subsequent cooling of enthusiasm for structured finance had on the development of the crisis as it unfolded. Rating agencies have been viewed on Wall Street as reluctant to anticipate change in credit quality, slow to act when

---

43. Besedovsky also discusses the role of Clarkson in these terms. Natalia Besedovsky, "Financialization as Calculative Practice: The Rise of Structured Finance and the Cultural and Calculative Transformation of Credit Rating Agencies," *Socio-Economic Review* 16, no. 1 (2018): 75.

things start to deteriorate, but then, to safeguard their reputations, eager to engage in widespread downgrading of ratings when things get worse. In 2006, the agencies downgraded structured finance instruments 885 times. In 2007 this number grew to 6,801, and in 2008 to 29,545.[44] But the 2008 figure actually represents a lower percentage of downgrades (6.7) than the year before (7.2) because the market was larger.[45] Moreover, when compared with 2002 (4.1) and 2003 (5.1), the percentage of downgrades is not radically different, but in a market that is 54 percent of its size in 2008.[46]

Even if the downgrading activity in 2008 cooled off slightly in percentage terms, the absolute number was huge and historically unprecedented. It seems reasonable then to infer a pro-cyclical effect to rating downgrades in 2008, in the sense that these actions by the rating agencies may have made the situation worse by escalating crisis sentiment among investors.[47] Roger Lowenstein highlights what he calls Bernanke's "conundrum" over the link between widespread financial disaster and the reality of the relatively small number and low value of subprime loans. The solution to the conundrum, according to Bernanke, is understanding that subprime structured finance was a "trigger," not a cause of the crisis. This trigger led investors to become uncertain about the value of opaque securities and run from the market in panic.[48] We can apply the same triggering logic to rating downgrades in 2008. They made market

44. Efraim Benmelech and Jennifer Dlugosz, "The Credit Rating Crisis," in *NBER Macroeconomics Annual 2009*, ed. Daron Acemoglu, Kenneth Rogoff, and Michael Woodford (Chicago: University of Chicago Press, 2010), 171.

45. Benmelech and Dlugosz, 170.

46. Benmelech and Dlugosz, 173.

47. Abdelal and Blyth, "Just Who Put You in Charge?," 47, 50.

48. Roger Lowenstein, *The End of Wall Street* (New York: Penguin, 2010), 107. Lowenstein suggests that Bernanke underestimated subprime and "related problems," which, in his estimation, were "surely more than a 'trigger.'"

sentiment worse at the time. In different circumstances, when confidence was higher and uncertainty lower, the impact of those downgrades might have been much less consequential than it was.

Repo

A key phenomenon, missed by most observers at the time of the crisis, has come into sharper focus in recent appraisals. This is the role of repurchase agreements, or repo, in magnifying the escalating market uncertainty in 2007 and 2008 into a truly massive event with global ramifications.[49] Structured finance was not itself ground zero for the global financial crisis, despite the many thousands of words that have been written about this financial innovation. The thing that tore everything up, that caused the panic, was the use of structured finance in the repo markets, the "true heart" of the global financial crisis.[50] Earlier in this book I discussed disintermediation, and how banks have come under pressure from more efficient, and thus cheaper, capital markets. Repo is the twin-turbo V8 version of disintermediation, in which investment banks bor-

---

49. Daniela Gabor, "The (Impossible) Repo Trinity: The Political Economy of Repo Markets," *Review of International Political Economy* 23, no. 6 (2016): 967–1000.

50. Adam Tooze, *Crashed: How a Decade of Financial Crises Changed the World* (London: Allen Lane, 2018), 60. For a broad critique of Tooze, see Perry Anderson, "Situationism à l'Envers?," *New Left Review* 119 (September-October 2019): 47–93. Also see Cédric Durand, "In the Crisis Cockpit," *New Left Review* 116/117 (March-June 2019): 201–212. Barry Eichengreen has written another, very substantial, history of the crisis, placing recent events in historical perspective. See his *Hall of Mirrors: The Great Depression, the Great Recession, and the Uses—and Abuses—of History* (New York: Oxford University Press, 2015). Also see Philip Mirowski, *Never Let a Serious Crisis Go to Waste: How Neoliberalism Survived the Financial Meltdown* (London: Verso, 2013); John Cassidy, *How Markets Fail: The Logic of Economic Calamities* (London: Allen Lane, 2009); and Cédric Durand, *Fictitious Capital: How Finance Is Appropriating Our Future*, trans. David Broder (London: Verso, 2017).

row money short-term (often overnight) to fund their proprietary trading activities. Traditionally, the repo markets have put a premium on very high quality collateral to secure those loans, and the collateral of choice has been US Treasuries (bills and bonds), because of their unmatched credit quality. But as the repo markets developed, other securities, including structured financings, started to be used as collateral.

Gabor notes that the repo market has two segments, a bilateral segment, where institutions lend to each other directly, and a tri-party segment, where the management of the collateral is done by a third party.[51] Legal changes concerning the treatment of collateral in 2005 destabilized repo by allowing the use of lower-rated asset-backed securities as collateral, although government debt remained two-thirds of both the US and European repo markets, worth about $20 trillion in 2008.[52]

Tooze describes how repo allowed investment banks to grow their balance sheets.[53] The risk of this, as he suggests, is that you might not have your funding "rolled over" if your institution recently made major losses.[54] The same might occur if there were doubts about your collateral. Lehman funded 50 percent of its $691 billion balance sheet via repo at the end of fiscal year 2007. For Goldman Sachs, Merrill Lynch, and Morgan Stanley the figure was 40 percent. Repo was at the core of the business model of these investment banks, and they could not survive without this funding.[55]

As the crisis developed in 2007, Tooze notes how Bear Stearns was shut out of the commercial paper market. What is a surprise,

---

51. Gabor, "The (Impossible) Repo Trinity," 968.
52. Gabor, 969.
53. Tooze, *Crashed*, 60–62.
54. Tooze, 62.
55. Tooze, 62.

given that repo was "fully collateralized lending," was that a "run on repo" developed too.[56] In early March 2008 Bear could raise $100 billion overnight, via the repo market. By March 13 it could not roll over $14 billion. Then things became much worse as uncertainty spread to the entire system.[57] The tri-party market, overseen by JPMorgan Chase and Bank of New York Mellon, remained open to strong counterparties with top-quality collateral, such as US Treasuries and GSE-backed mortgage securities. But the bilateral repo market, where private label (non-GSE) asset-backed securities were used as securities, became more and more difficult to access.[58] The months between March and September 2008 saw Lehman's experience deteriorating access to repo, and by September 12 Lehman's were unable to roll over their repo borrowings or secure other support, declaring bankruptcy on September 15.[59]

In 2011, at a hearing by the Subcommittee on Oversight and Investigations of the US House of Representatives, Congressman Brad Miller of North Carolina observed:

> What really happened in September of 2008 was described in the press as interbank lending freezing up. And in fairness to the press, it is going to be pretty hard to explain it any more deeply than that.
>
> But in a part of the shadow banking system that hardly any American knows anything about, hardly anyone in Congress knows anything about, and those who know something about it don't know very much, was the repo market. And as much money was moving around every night in the repo market as there was in bank deposits.

---

56. Tooze, 147.
57. Tooze, 148.
58. Tooze, 149.
59. Tooze, 149.

Bear Stearns was getting $70 billion a night in repo market lending, every night. What they were doing with that money was making longer-term loans. Using very short-term borrowing for longer-term loans is not a formula for financial stability. And what happened was that there was an old-fashioned run, like what you saw in, "It's a Wonderful Life," that used to happen to depository institutions before there was deposit insurance[,] in the repo market.[60]

Repo was gigantic, with $2.5 trillion in collateral posted on a daily basis, just prior to the Lehman collapse in just the tri-party segment.[61] It also proved to be very fragile once it no longer behaved according to expectations. Tooze has characterized the market as "bimodal."[62] One day repo functioned as a "gigantic trillion-dollar machine based on confidence and widely acceptable collateral."[63] The next day even major market participants could be shut out. This is Randall Germain's "great freeze," when finance became "operationally dysfunctional," nearly bringing the global economy to its knees.[64] In September 2019, problems in the repo markets induced what *The Economist* called a "cold sweat," raising fears of a "reprise" of the global financial crisis, forcing the Federal Reserve to inject funds into the banking system to ease liquidity.[65]

---

60. Brad Miller, "Oversight of the Credit Rating Agencies Post–Dodd-Frank," Subcommittee on Oversight and Investigations of the Committee on Financial Services, US House of Representatives, July 27, 2011, 14, https://www.govinfo.gov/content/pkg/CHRG-112hhrg67946/pdf/CHRG-112hhrg67946.pdf, accessed August 28, 2019.
61. Tooze, *Crashed*, 150.
62. Tooze, 150.
63. Tooze, 150.
64. Randall Germain, *Global Politics and Financial Governance* (London: Palgrave Macmillan, 2010), 79.
65. *The Economist*, "Rep uh oh," September 28, 2019, 88. Also see "Making the World Go Round," *The Economist*, November 2, 2019, 73.

THE FINANCIAL MECHANISMS I discussed in this chapter are fascinating and shocking. The ambition and intellectual boldness of structured finance is eye-opening. The massiveness of repo, and how it has become central to finance, is gripping. Finance really is that aggressive, self-confident, and determined. The problem is that financial instruments are ultimately not technical things. They are not like the drives in your computer or the air conditioning in your car. Financial instruments exist in a social world, like poker, where people use them to pursue their ambitions and to avert their fears, looking to others all the time, wondering what they will do, "dancing," as Chuck Prince suggested at the start of the chapter. This is something participants are compelled to do, he suggests, "as long as the music is playing." But our expectations that finance is a machine, a game of chance like roulette, that we can design effective technical and legal fixes to make the game work for us, come unstuck as the reality of the poker game asserts itself in the right circumstances. These are the social foundations of global finance playing out. When repo turns out to be like a poker game our whole world can be turned upside down.

5

Cogs in the Wheel of Financial Destruction

> Well, I think they were wrong like everybody else.
> [LAUGH] . . . People pay attention to ratings, and
> they had a model. . . . I've never seen the model, but
> it must have said that . . . house prices—residential
> house prices can't take a dive, and that they won't
> take a dive all over the country.
>
> That was a fallacious model, it was held by Freddie
> Mac, Fannie Mae, the U.S. Congress, the media,
> me, [LAUGH] investors, and—and home buyers all
> over. . . . It was part of a bubble mentality, and that
> bubble mentality got incorporated into . . . models
> used by not only rating agencies, but others.
> —*Warren E. Buffett, CEO, Berkshire Hathaway,*
> *CNBC, June 2, 2010*

Why did the agencies risk their franchise by switching to an advisory role, telling clients what they needed, and helping issuers obtain the ratings they required to create their structured finance products? What we need to get to grips with is what dislocated a long-entrenched conservative rating mentality, a system and set of habits that had been established in these Wall Street institutions for decades. The context for what happened is the disintermediation of finance in which borrowers seek funds in the capital markets directly, rather than borrowing from banks.[1] Disintermediation mobilized banks to pursue securitized finance. RMBS offered higher returns to the banks, but with the alluring prospect of strong credit ratings.

Why did the agencies accept their changed role in securitized finance, even at the risk of destroying their rating franchise? My argument is that after the Enron disaster the agencies were uncertain about the rating business. They did not know what disasters lay around the next corner, given financial innovation.[2] Their old model of how to operate no longer seemed relevant in these circumstances. The Enron rating failure highlighted the weakness of the approach to rating taken by the agencies, which struggled to keep up with the rapid pace of financial innovation Enron had fully exploited in the 1990s. Talking to this senior Moody's executive, in the now-demolished Dun and Bradstreet building at 99 Church Street, next to the dusty ruins of the World Trade Center, I learnt how Moody's was eager to find out what the market wanted from ratings after Enron.[3] Moody's had, she suggested, asked market participants whether they wanted ratings to incorporate stock market data about corporations, allowing ratings to be updated on an hourly basis. The reaction to this, I was told, was negative. Although market participants wanted ratings to be timely, they saw ratings as quite different from immediate market judgments such as those revealed by a stock price. Ratings were not as ephem-

---

1. Rethel and Sinclair, *The Problem with Banks*, 51–70.
2. This was a feature of my discussions with a senior Moody's official in March 2002, in the wake of Enron and the collapse of the World Trade Center twin towers, which were adjacent to Moody's New York headquarters.
3. Jenny Wiggins and Peter Spiegel, "Enron's Fall May Spark Credit Rating Rethink," *Financial Times*, January 19–20, 2002, 1.

eral as this. For me, the idea that Moody's, still a bastion of conservative thinking on Wall Street in 2002, was asking the market how Moody's should change was shocking. It revealed a new level of anxiety in the company I had not encountered in the previous decade of research on rating. Perhaps the postapocalyptic atmosphere just outside the building made this worse, but what came across very clearly in this interview was that the dynamism of finance presented Moody's with a world where unexpected events and challenges were lying in wait under every rock, as in a novel by Joan Didion. These shocks could be fatal, as Arthur Andersen, Enron's auditor, had recently found out. This official saw these possibilities as requiring new thinking, and a more robust company. Moody's went on a program of acquiring quantitatively-driven credit analysis start-ups starting around this time and continuing to today, as have the other members of the Big Three, just as other corporations such as General Electric have bought out other companies when they have sought a new technology or to enter a new area of business activity.[4] These acquisitions seem to be about making sure the core business of rating remains up to date, and does not simply find itself outmoded by change such as that which befell typing pools and mainframe word processors like those manufactured by Wang Laboratories when personal computers became a business tool on every desk.

Compounding this acute uncertainty inside the rating agencies in the early 2000s was the rise of Fitch. Although we know Fitch as a member of the Big Three, this did not become a reality until after 2000. Before this, from Fitch's founding in 1913 until the 1990s,

---

4. For example, Fitch sold a risk analytics firm to IBM in late 2011. "IBM to Acquire Algorithmics," press release, September 1, 2011, https://www-03.ibm .com/press/us/en/pressrelease/35176.wss, accessed September 5, 2020.

Fitch had been much smaller than Moody's and S&P, although it created the rating scale licensed by S&P and was respected for municipal rating in the US market. In the 1990s, Fitch merged with IBCA, a London-based agency, and with Duff & Phelps of Chicago and Thomson Bank Watch in 2000. The new company, which has been wholly owned by Hearst Corporation since 2018, is now comparable in size to Moody's and S&P. Building on a long-developed, reputable brand and serious new financing, Fitch became a constituent member of the newly christened Big Three, while other, newer agencies without Fitch's long time on Wall Street or influx of cash have not achieved either recognition or business growth.[5] In 1997 Fitch issued less than one in ten ratings. By 2007, Fitch was issuing one-third of all ratings.[6]

At the same time as Fitch was expanding into this new status the stakes of the game were growing too. When I first went to New York for field work in 1992 I met the president of S&P in his office with a panoramic view of the harbor. Even then it was obvious from his comments that structured finance was an enticing new development as far as rating agency revenue growth was concerned. From nothing in 1990 to around half of revenue just prior to the global financial crisis, the rise and rise of structured finance was also changing the face of the capital markets and of the rating business.

Before the recapitalization that produced the modern Fitch, rating was a comfortable duopoly, with modest revenue growth. But this changed as the 1990s unfolded. Fitch transformed a comfort-

---

5. A former Moody's official first suggested to me that the reemergence of Fitch was a key element in changes in the ratings market and changes in how Moody's did business.

6. B. Becker and T. Milbourn, "How Did Increased Competition Affect Credit Ratings?," *Journal of Financial Economics* 101 (2011): 494.

able duopoly into a three-way oligopoly. As Becker and Milbourn suggest, "A broad consensus exists among policy makers and regulators around the potential benefits of increasing competition between ratings providers as a tool of improving ratings quality."[7] Because most securities typically need two ratings, one of what has become the Big Three was going to lose each time a rating was required. What made each of the Big Three acutely sensitive to this is the stakes involved. Shrinking market share meant less access to the revenues from structured finance issues, making market share matter more than ever, changing the agencies forever.

Bo Becker and Todd Milbourn's work has demonstrated that increased competition in the rating market with the entry of the third major rating agency, Fitch, is "unequivocally consistent with lower ratings quality as competition increased."[8] Competition seems to weaken "reputational incentives for providing quality in the ratings industry."[9] Encouraging competition may reduce the price of ratings but will harm the veracity of the product itself. Becker and Milbourn suggest that "quality in the ratings industry relies on rents that reward reputation-building activities, which are costly in the short run. The reduction of such rents reduces the amount of reputation-building, i.e., high quality production."[10] If Fitch had not managed to become a member of what became the Big Three, the agencies may have taken a more arm's-length relationship to structured finance, and it may never have become the business it did.

———————

7. Becker and Milbourn, 494.
8. Becker and Milbourn, 496.
9. Becker and Milbourn, 499.
10. Becker and Milbourn, 499.

Scrutiny of the Agencies

US lawmakers convened hearings to investigate the role of the rating agencies in the financial crisis on several occasions starting in 2007. Hearings were held by committees and subcommittees of the Senate and the House of Representatives. Congressional hearings into the rating agencies long predated the financial crisis. The most recent investigations prior to the crisis occurred around the Enron collapse and the process of creating the Rating Agency Reform Act that became law in September 2006.

A year or so after passage of the Rating Agency Reform Act, and following the summer 2007 RMBS rating downgrades, the Committee on Banking, Housing, and Urban Affairs of the US Senate held a hearing on September 26, 2007, into the "role and impact of the credit rating agencies on the subprime credit markets."[11] Senator Jack Reed, acting as chairman of the hearing, observed that the recent wave of downgrades had "caused some investors to lose confidence in both the integrity and reliability of these ratings."[12] But, he suggests, "our goal is to strike the right balance between voluntary and regulatory actions" so as to restore confidence.[13] When Chairman Christopher Cox of the SEC observed in his statement that the Rating Agency Reform Act does not provide the power to question particular ratings or alter procedures or methodologies, Reed asked him if he wanted those powers. Cox answered, "It is very easy to see in the abstract what would become of competition,

11. "The Role and Impact of the Credit Rating Agencies on the Subprime Credit Markets," www.govinfo.gov/content/pkg/CHRG-110shrg50357/pdf/CHRG -110shrg50357.pdf, accessed December 12, 2018.

12. "Opening Statement of Senator Jack Reed," in "Role and Impact of the Credit Rating Agencies," 1, accessed December 18, 2018.

13. "Opening Statement of Senator Jack Reed," 2.

what would become of the market, what would become of the substance of the ratings themselves if they just disintegrated into following a Government regulation on how to do it. There would be no innovation. There would be no potential for improvement. Or at least there would be a real collar on that because we would have determined a priori."[14] Subsequently, Cox refers to the remedial effects of competition in the ratings industry, assumed in the Reform Act. Senator Richard Shelby, the ranking member, suggests to Cox that "there is no substitute for transparency and competition," to which Cox agrees.[15] Continuing this concern with the impact of the supply of information, Senator John E. Sununu asks Cox whether data on historical default rates is available, to "compare performance from one [rating] organization to another."[16]

John C. Coffee, professor of law at Columbia University, sought to "paint a picture of the gatekeeper in this market who is under great pressure" in his evidence to the committee.[17] He suggested that structured finance was different from other securities, because it empowered different parties and therefore put pressure on ratings. This was "because structured finance gives new power to the investment banks. They are assembling large pools of securitized assets. They are repeat players. And they can remove their business if they do not get what they like. They have much more power than the traditional corporation."[18] He went on to note that when

---

14. "Statement of Christopher D. Cox, Chairman, Securities and Exchange Commission," in "Role and Impact of the Credit Rating Agencies," 16, accessed December 18, 2018.

15. "Statement of Christopher D. Cox," 19.

16. "Statement of Christopher D. Cox," 21.

17. "Statement of John C. Coffee, Professor of Law, Columbia University," in "Role and Impact of the Credit Rating Agencies," 27, accessed December 18, 2018.

18. "Statement of John C. Coffee," 27.

Moody's downgraded a series of RMBS securities in July 2007, their market share of these CDOs fell from 75 percent to just 25 percent. As he saw it, this equates to "extreme pressure" on Moody's, undermining ratings quality.[19]

Senator Reed then asked questions of Vickie Tillman, head of rating at S&P in 2007. When Reed suggests that the agencies were not just rating RMBS but that they were also "helping structure them or advising the client as to what they could do" with the securities, Tillman responded:

> First of all, I would like to make a point clear, that our criteria is absolutely transparent to all of those in the marketplace. They understand it. They see it. The models that we use internally to look at the stress testing or look at the probability defaults around the loans that are packaged in these, these are readily available in the marketplace, as well.
>
> . . . There is a lot of understanding around what kind of loan characteristics, what kind of stressing we do in the marketplace.
>
> . . . As the originator originates the loan, the investment banker works with the originator to package the loan. They already have an idea of what kind of loans they are looking for, relative to the way Standard & Poor's looks at the almost 70 different characteristics, if you will, on every loan that is put in a pool.
>
> Once that is packaged, I think there seems to be a point that needs to be made, that this is actually a very sophisticated investment community. Most of these bonds, if not a majority of them, are sold to institutional investors or had been sold to hedge funds who have their own staffs that not only look at ratings, which again is only speaking to credit risk. But the ratings [do] not speak to suitability of the investment, the pricing of the investment. They have their own firms there, their own people that run their models. Or they use our models as a benchmark and run their own propri-

---

19. "Statement of John C. Coffee," 28.

etary models before they will make a decision as to whether that is an appropriate investment for a particular risk appetite.

. . . They go through that process and they present to Standard & Poor's a package of pooled securities.[20]

Senator Reed then interjected:

Senator Reed: So there is no collaboration between Standard & Poor's and the issuer, in terms of how the product is structured? That you simply take what they present you, evaluate it, and give a rating?

Ms. Tillman: We have a great dialog. We have an open dialog with the investment bankers. They need to understand what our criteria is. We need to understand better what their structure is. And if we tell them that it does not fit with our criteria, what we do is tell them why it does not fit with our criteria—

Senator Reed: And how to make it fit.

Ms. Tillman: No, sir. We do not tell them how to make it better. That is up to them to make the determination as to whether they want to change the structure, change the pool, change the overcollateralization.

Senator Reed: I appreciate that . . . I think, at least on the surface, there is a suggestion here that there is something going on more than simply being presented a group of loans or a product, here is our rating, take it or leave it. There is this dialog.[21]

The October 22, 2008, hearing of the Committee on Oversight and Government Reform of the US House of Representatives took place

---

20. "Statement of Vickie A. Tillman, Executive Vice President for Credit Market Services, Standard & Poor's," in "Role and Impact of the Credit Rating Agencies," 34, accessed December 18, 2018.

21. "Statement of Vickie A. Tillman," 35. Carruthers documents the "active collaboration" between the agencies and prospective issuers of structured finance securities. See Carruthers, "Knowledge and Liquidity," 166.

a few weeks after the collapse of Lehman Brothers, government assumption of control over Fannie Mae and Freddie Mac, and the $180 billion US government bailout (and 80 percent ownership) of the bond insurer AIG.[22] It featured statements and testimony by, and questioning of, insiders such as Raymond W. McDaniel Jr., chairman and chief executive officer of Moody's Corporation (parent of Moody's Investors Service), and former insiders (now critical voices) including Jerome Fons, a former managing director at Moody's. In questioning witnesses, the committee made use of documents (including e-mails) they had obtained under subpoena from the rating agencies.

In particular, the committee chairman, Representative Waxman, made use of a transcript of a managing director–level "town hall" meeting held at Moody's on September 11, 2007.[23] Waxman highlighted the town hall meeting because it revealed much inner turmoil at Moody's and the struggle over market share that lay behind this. What Waxman did not mention was McDaniel's comments from his presentation about how the regulators were looking to Moody's for assistance:

> We need you, Moody's, we need you, the ratings industry, to come up with your own credible answers to solving what's going on in the subprime market and with the credit crunch because, if you don't, then it's going to move into the political sphere, and there's going to be blunt instrument kind of reactions. Overreaching regulation becomes . . . a risk. And the regulators were saying, frankly we'd rather you come up with a solution because it's going to be better than

---

22. "Credit Rating Agencies and the Financial Crisis," www.gpo.gov/fdsys/pkg/CHRG-110hhrg51103/pdf/CHRG-110hhrg51103.pdf, accessed December 3, 2018.

23. Moody's Investors Service, Managing Director's Town Hall meeting, https://democratsoversight.house.gov/sites/democrats.oversight.house.gov/files/documents/20081022112343.pdf, accessed December 3, 2018.

what the politicians can come up with. And in effect, inviting us to give them the tools to help respond to a lot of the accusations that are going on.[24]

Under questioning, the S&P representative (president of S&P, Deven Sharma) insisted his organization did not assist issuers to design asset-backed securities so they would achieve a specific rating.[25] He suggested that analysts could not advise issuers on structuring of deals, although they do offer an opinion on whether deals brought to them meet their criteria for a specific rating or not. McDaniel said Moody's did discuss with issuers and investors possible ratings for financial instruments in advance of their being offered for sale. Stephen Joynt, CEO and president of Fitch, asserted that consulting and designing securities was not part of their job, but that the process was necessarily "iterative."

A year before these hearings, the *Wall Street Journal* ran an article that discussed the iterative nature of the rating of structured finance. They characterized the interaction in this process as "collaboration" between the underwriters putting the securities together and the rating agencies: "Underwriters don't just assemble a security out of home loans and ship it off to the credit raters to see what grade it gets. Instead, they work with rating companies while designing a mortgage bond or other security, making sure it gets high-enough ratings to be marketable."[26] Ritholtz notes, citing the same article, that the agencies "were active participants in

---

24. Moody's Investors Service, Managing Director's Town Hall meeting, 4.

25. These interactions are on pages 163 and 164 of "Credit Rating Agencies and the Financial Crisis," accessed December 3, 2018.

26. Aaron Lucchetti and Serena Ng, "How Rating Firms' Calls Fueled Subprime Mess," *Wall Street Journal*, https://www.wsj.com/articles/SB118714461352698015, accessed November 25, 2019.

the creation of the structured products—not objective third-party arbiters who merely *misunderestimated* their creditworthiness."[27]

On conflicts of interest, the hearing highlighted the pressures the agencies were under to retain market share, especially with questions from Representative Carolyn B. Maloney of New York, using an October 23, 2007, document obtained from Moody's that helped to highlight the difficulties. Quoting from the letter by McDaniel, Maloney notes concerns about divergent issuer and investor interests in ratings as penalizing quality of the rating product to the extent that "unchecked competition on this basis can place the entire financial system at risk."[28] Earlier in the day, at the first session, when Maloney had introduced this communication between McDaniel and the Moody's board, she quoted this document on the tension between different stakeholders in ratings: "Moody's for years has struggled with this dilemma. On the one hand, we need to win the business and maintain market share or we cease to be relevant. On the other hand, our reputation depends on maintaining ratings quality."[29]

Later in the session, Representative John F. Tierney of Massachusetts asks the rating agency CEOs if abandoning issuer pays and returning to the investor pays business model would alleviate the

---

27. Ritholtz, *Bailout Nation*, 112. Misunderestimated, as used by Ritholtz, is an example of a "Bushism," created by President George W. Bush.

28. "Credit Rating Agencies and the Financial Crisis," 165, accessed December 3, 2018.

29. The quote comes from a document placed on the committee record by Maloney. "Credit Policy Issues at Moody's Suggested by the Subprime/Liquidity Crisis," attached to an e-mail of Raymond McDaniel of October 21, 2007. The quote read in by Maloney appears on page 60 of "Credit Rating Agencies and the Financial Crisis," accessed December 10, 2018. The document appears on pages 61–65 of the Committee transcript.

stresses highlighted by Maloney.[30] While he and Joynt agreed stresses existed, McDaniel observed:

> I think the biggest mistake we could make is believing that an investor pay model does not embed conflicts of interest. So as long as rating agencies are paid by any party with a financial stake in the outcome of our opinions, and that includes investors and issuers, there are going to be pressures. And so the question is not are there conflicts of interest? There are. It's managing them properly and managing them with enough transparency that regulatory authorities and market participants can conclude that, in fact, those conflicts are being handled to the right professional standard.[31]

Some years later, at a hearing of the Treasury Committee of the House of Commons in London, Paul Taylor, the new CEO and president of Fitch, was asked about the conflict of interest issue by Pat McFadden, MP:

> *Mr. McFadden*: It is the seller of the product who pays the fee. Does that not create a conflict of interest with the seller paying the person who is expressing a rating opinion on his product for the investor market?[32]
>
> *Paul Taylor*: Yes, it does create a conflict of interest. I think the key thing is to recognise that conflict of interest and to manage it. Any other business model you could come up with would have a conflict of interest, so if investors pay they have an interest in

30. "Credit Rating Agencies and the Financial Crisis," 169, accessed December 4, 2018.

31. "Credit Rating Agencies and the Financial Crisis," 169.

32. The quotations that follow are from Oral Evidence before the Treasury Committee, "Inquiry into Credit Rating Agencies," House of Commons, March 7, 2012. This is the uncorrected transcript (there is no corrected transcript), https://publications.parliament.uk/pa/cm201012/cmselect/cmtreasy/uc1866-ii/uc186601.htm, accessed November 7, 2019 (unpaginated).

whether we are rating up, rating down, or keeping it the same, because there are many types of investors. Many are short-term trading investors, so there could be a conflict with investors. If some kind of central government body is assigning ratings, there would be a potential conflict there; would it downgrade the nation's banks when it needs to?

So there will always be a conflict in whatever model you choose. You have to manage the conflicts. I think with the issuer pays model, it has been scrutinised so much over the last seven years in particular that there are a whole raft of issues put in place now to manage and to disclose those conflicts.

Mr. McFadden: Explain to me why there is a conflict if the investor pays.

Paul Taylor: I own a bond and I am thinking of selling my bond, so if there is going to be a rating action on that bond it could influence the price of it. So if I can influence the decision as to whether it goes up, down or stays the same I may have an interest in it.

Mr. McFadden: Across the industry, if you recognise that there is a conflict of interest in the issuer pays model that you all use, has there been any cross-industry discussion or is there a deep internal discussion, say in your firm, about, "Could we come up with something else? We admit there is a conflict of interest here. Could we come up with something else that would give greater market confidence about who pays us and how we earn our fees?"

Paul Taylor: We have had those discussions internally. We can't come up with a solution that allows us to keep the scale of activity we have, to have the breadth of coverage we have, and to have the independence that we have. The issuer pays model is understood, it is accepted. When you talk about improving market confidence, I think the market still has confidence in credit rating agencies in the work they do. We are still used by people; they still talk to us on a regular basis. I think they are a bit wiser now in terms of using other sources as well, there is less blind faith, but we still have perfectly good discussions with the market.

More recently, Ian Linnell, now president of Fitch Ratings, agreed with Paul Taylor, now president and CEO of Fitch Group (which includes Fitch Ratings), telling me that "all business models have potential conflicts of interest," and that in their experience neither investors nor issuers sought a change back to the "investor pays" model.[33]

Understanding of structured finance among committee members was sometimes strong during the October 22, 2008, hearing of the Committee on Oversight and Government Reform of the U.S. House of Representatives. But at times their lack of understanding of how structured finance worked mirrored that of the general public. Representative Diane E. Watson of California, after asking questions about California public finance and bond issuance, commented on the "seemingly arbitrary meaning of credit ratings" and asked how people "are supposed to trust these ratings when junk bonds based on subprime mortgages receive AAA ratings, the same rating as the Federal Treasury."[34]

At the end of the hearing, Chairman Waxman brought the meeting to a conclusion by quoting some of the memorable phrases from the rating agency documents obtained by the committee, suggesting that these revealed a "complete breakdown" in the agencies:[35] "We drink the Kool-Aid." "Fitch and S&P went nuts." "No one cared because the machine just kept going." "We sold our soul to the devil for revenue." "It could be structured by cows, and we would rate it." "Let's hope we are all retired by the time this house of cards falters." "Any requests for loan level tapes is totally unreasonable."[36]

---

33. Interview with Ian Linnell, Global Analytical Head, Fitch Ratings, Canary Wharf, London, October 2, 2014.
34. "Credit Rating Agencies and the Financial Crisis," 185, accessed December 4, 2018.
35. "Credit Rating Agencies and the Financial Crisis," 192.
36. "Credit Rating Agencies and the Financial Crisis," 191.

Among other things, Waxman's reference to the "structured by cows" quote is curious. This line had been brought to the committee's attention in the first session that morning by Representative John A. Yarmuth of Kentucky. It was contained in an instant message between two employees in the S&P structured finance division. The discussion was about whether S&P should rate a particular deal. The wording of this conversation was reported in the hearing minutes as follows:

> *Official one*: "That deal is ridiculous."
>
> *Official two*: "I know, right model definitely does not capture half the risk."
>
> *Official one*: "We should not be rating it."
>
> *Official two*: "We rate every deal it could be structured by cows and we would rate it."
>
> *Official one*: "But there is a lot of risk associated with it. I personally don't feel comfy signing off as a committee member."[37]

The reference to cows hit the headlines. What was not reported was the S&P CEO's clarification that the full context of the message revealed that the analysts were referring to bank models, not S&P models, and that these models were subsequently revised before ratings were made. Yarmuth acknowledged that the out-of-context quote may have distorted its meaning, but suggested the revision process "sounds pretty suspicious."[38]

Perhaps the most intensely resourced hearing ever undertaken into the rating agencies took place on April 23, 2010, by the Permanent Subcommittee on Investigations of the US Senate Committee on Homeland Security and Governmental Affairs. Senator

---

37. "Credit Rating Agencies and the Financial Crisis," 175.
38. "Credit Rating Agencies and the Financial Crisis," 175.

Carl Levin of Michigan chaired this hearing, which drew on hundreds of pages of e-mails and other documents obtained from the rating agencies.[39]

Using language similar to Bernanke's, Levin refers to ratings downgrades as a "trigger" to the financial crisis:

> Looking back, if any single event can be identified as the immediate trigger of the 2008 financial crisis, my vote would be for the mass downgrades starting in July 2007, when the credit rating agencies realized that their AAA ratings would not hold. . . . Those mass downgrades hit the markets like a hammer.[40]

Underlying this trigger is, he suggests, financial innovation, saying the sort of mortgages the agencies were rating in the years leading up to the crisis presented problems. Traditional, low-risk, thirty-year mortgages were displaced by new mortgages. In these cases, "The credit rating agencies simply did not have data on how these higher-risk mortgages would perform over time."[41] Levin then describes the process in which the agencies realize their assumptions are wrong, decide they need to revise their models, but prevaricate about applying those new assumptions to existing ratings in 2005 and 2006:[42]

---

39. The subcommittee subsequently published a book on their findings: United States Senate Permanent Subcommittee on Investigations, Committee on Homeland Security and Governmental Affairs, *Wall Street and the Financial Crisis: Anatomy of a Financial Collapse* (St. Petersburg, FL: Red and Black, 2011). Also see Elise J. Bean, *Financial Exposure: Carl Levin's Senate Investigations into Finance and Tax Abuse* (New York: Palgrave Macmillan, 2018).

40. "Opening Statement of Senator Levin," in "Wall Street and the Financial Crisis: The Role of the Credit Rating Agencies," 5, www.govinfo.gov/content/pkg /CHRG-111shrg57321/pdf/CHRG-111shrg57321.pdf, accessed December 20, 2018.

41. "Opening Statement of Senator Levin," 5–6.

42. "Opening Statement of Senator Levin," 6.

The revised RMBS model projected much higher default rates for high-risk mortgages and required greater protections against loss, including 40 percent more credit protection for BBB-graded subprime securities. That meant a 40-percent larger cushion to protect against losses. Re-evaluating existing RMBS securities with the revised model would likely have led to downgrades, angry issuers, and even angrier investors, so S&P did not do it. Moody's did not either; after strengthening its RMBS model to issue new ratings, it chose not to apply it to existing securities.[43]

When the agencies do finally apply these new assumptions after the housing market enters free fall, downgrades follow in summer 2007.

Summing up the content of the information obtained by subpoena from the rating agencies, Levin observed:

The documents . . . show how the crushing volume of ratings undermined the ratings process. Despite record profits, both credit rating agencies were understaffed and overwhelmed with complex deals that investment bankers wanted to close within days. The documents show how investment bankers argued with the credit rating analysts, substituted worse assets at the last minute, and pressured analysts to waive their procedures and standards. We even saw instances of bankers pushing to remove analysts who were not playing ball.[44]

These documents, and the hearing witnesses, suggest, said Levin, that the rating "environment changed from an academic culture focused on accurate ratings to one of intense pressure to get the deals done and preserve market share."[45]

---

43. "Opening Statement of Senator Levin," 6.
44. "Opening Statement of Senator Levin," 7.
45. "Opening Statement of Senator Levin," 7.

Subsequently, Eric Kolchinsky, a former senior manager in the Moody's derivatives group, noted that in the first half of 2007 his group alone generated $200 million in revenue for Moody's. In his estimation, this was about one-fifth of total revenue generated by the agency during this period.[46] This revenue came with a price:

> The incentives in the market for rating agency services favored, and still favor, short-term profit over credit quality and quantity over quality.
>
> At Moody's, the source of this conflict was the quest for market share. Managers of rating groups were expected by their supervisors to build, or at least maintain, market share. It was an unspoken understanding that loss of market share would cause a manager to lose his or her job. . . . While, to my knowledge, senior management never explicitly forced the lowering of credit standards, it was one easy way for a managing director to regain market share.[47]

The motivations in the agencies were so confused by the mid-2000s that raters no longer seemed to think of their traditional principals as their clients anymore:

> *Senator Levin*: Who basically did your agency think was the client? Was it the investment banker or was it the investor? Mr. Kolchinsky.
>
> *Mr. Kolchinsky*: It was the banker. The bankers were typically referred to as clients. If an investor called, they would be clients, but they never did. It was just simply the bankers, and they were the clients.[48]

---

46. "Testimony of Eric Kolchinsky, Former Team Managing Director, Structured Derivative Products Group, Moody's Investors Service," in "Wall Street and the Financial Crisis," 15, accessed December 28, 2018.

47. "Testimony of Eric Kolchinsky," 14–15.

48. "Wall Street and the Financial Crisis," 44, accessed December 28, 2018.

Senior management at Moody's suggested to witness Richard Michalek, former senior vice president for structured derivatives at Moody's, when issuers complained about him, Moody's were trying to take a longer view of the rating process when dealing with aggressive, deal-hungry bankers: "When I had some discussions with Brian Clarkson about the process, his perspective was, yes, we could effectively produce perfect ratings, but we would not be on the deals. And if we are not on the deals, then we are not able to add any value whatsoever. So in some sense, it is like, yes, we take a little bit of this poison, but we are going to save the patient because you have the opportunity to get in there and fight the good fight."[49] In the third and final session of the hearing, Senator Levin, after hearing former and current senior executives at the agencies talk about how they are trying to make the rating process better, suggests that the future is not the point of the hearings. The subcommittee's task is primarily to investigate what went wrong and why. He discusses some of the exhibits gathered by the subcommittee and then refers back to Michalek's appearance earlier in the day:

> He testifies that the President of Moody's and the former head of Structured Finance, Brian Clarkson, who he believed was leading a change in culture at Moody's away from the more analytical environment to a profit-driven one, more to their customer, the investment bank, instead of the real customer, the investing public, but nonetheless what he says is that a number of bankers complained to Mr. Clarkson that Mr. Michalek was asking too many questions, doing too thorough a review. They wanted him removed from their deals, and they got their wish on future deals. Instead of rewarding Mr. Michalek for asking the probing questions and doing his job, he testified that Mr. Clarkson suggested that he provide an explanation for what he was doing and he ultimately was then not

---

49. "Wall Street and the Financial Crisis," 31.

allowed to work on deals with certain banks. That message is a pretty clear message to employees.[50]

In May 2009 the US congressional leadership established the Financial Crisis Inquiry Commission, chaired by Phil Angelides, former California state treasurer. The initial meeting of the commission took place September 2009, and the first public hearing occurred January 2010. The commission's hearing on the credit rating agencies, "Credibility of Credit Ratings, the Investment Decisions Made Based on Those Ratings, and the Financial Crisis," took place June 2, 2010, at the New School for Social Research in New York City.[51] The final report of the commission was published January 2011.[52]

Eric Kolchinsky, the former Moody's official, was first to testify. He reiterated many of the themes of his Washington testimony made in April to the subcommittee on investigations. He suggested that a "lack of guidance" from users of ratings meant "there's little concern that anyone would question the methods used to rate the products." The only thing Moody's had to worry about, he suggested, was "some amorphous concepts of reputational risk." He went on to note that "the rating agencies faced the age-old and pedestrian conflict between long-term product quality and short-term profits. They chose the latter."[53]

---

50. "Wall Street and the Financial Crisis," 91–92.

51. *Financial Crisis Inquiry Commission*, Official Transcript, Hearing on "Credibility of Credit Ratings, the Investment Decisions Made Based on Those Ratings, and the Financial Crisis," June 2, 2010, New School, New York, NY. Hereafter *Financial Crisis Inquiry Commission*, Official Transcript.

52. *The Financial Crisis Inquiry Report: Final Report of the National Commission on the Causes of the Financial and Economic Crisis in the United States* (New York: PublicAffairs, 2011).

53. Testimony of Eric Kolchinsky, *Financial Crisis Inquiry Commission*, Official Transcript, 20.

This led, he said, to a "shift of culture" from "one resembling a university academic department to one which values revenue at all costs." Management's focus on maintaining and expanding market share was fundamental to the change.[54] Kolchinsky also complained about the resources available to his group:

> Despite the increasing number of deals and the increasing complexity, our group did not receive adequate resources. By 2007, we were barely keeping up with the deal flow and the developments in the market. Many analysts, under pressure from bankers and their high deal loads, began to do the bare minimum of work required. We did not have the time to do any meaningful research into all the emerging credit issues. My own attempts to stay on top of the increasingly troubled market were chided by my manager. She told me that I spent too much time reading research.[55]

Later, during cross-examination, in response to a question from Commissioner Brooksley Born about lying by issuers or investment banks, Kolchinsky affirmed that

> for practical purposes, we would not walk away from a deal. We couldn't say no, so that would be the most obvious penalty, that you do in any normal business, if you find that your trading partner is not being truthful to you, you say, "I'm not going to do any business with you." So once that avenue is closed off because you want to increase market share, there's no penalty. We were in the position of being a quasi regulator, which means we had no power to compel people to give us information. We had no power to check the veracity of their statements.[56]

---

54. Testimony of Eric Kolchinsky, 20, 21.
55. Testimony of Eric Kolchinsky, 25.
56. Testimony of Eric Kolchinsky, 144–145.

Later in the day Warren Buffett, whose company Berkshire Hathaway was the largest single stockholder in Moody's at the time, appeared with Moody's CEO, McDaniel, to give testimony. Chairman Angelides probed him on the excellent financial performance of Moody's leading up to the crisis and whether this raised any red flags about Moody's. In reply, Buffett observed that he did not anticipate the scale of the housing bubble, and said that if he had "I probably would have sold my stock."[57] Buffett went on to suggest that in thinking about the housing market Moody's "made a mistake that virtually everybody in the country made."[58] Subsequently, he suggested that the size of the bubble was accentuated by off-balance-sheet financing and thus "hidden" from market view.[59] Angelides then suggested that the rating agencies had it too good, that "this system tilted in terms of lots of upside and no downside?" for the agencies. To which Buffett replied, "I think much of corporate America is tilted that way."[60] Elaborating on the question of competition in the rating business, Buffett noted how more competition might be bad:

> If there were ten rating agencies, all equally well regarded, all acceptable to the market, and you only needed one when Berkshire Hathaway issues a bond, we could have any one of them, those ten would compete either on price or laxity or both. I mean, they

57. Testimony of Warren Buffett, *Financial Crisis Inquiry Commission*, Official Transcript, 212–213. On the shortage of housing, see Kevin Erdmann, *Shut Out: How a Housing Shortage Caused the Great Recession and Crippled Our Economy* (Lanham, MD: Rowman and Littlefield, 2019). A broader analysis of these issues can be found in Herman M. Schwartz, *Subprime Nation: American Power, Global Capital, and the Housing Bubble* (Ithaca, NY: Cornell University Press, 2009).

58. Testimony of Warren Buffett, 213.

59. Testimony of Warren Buffett, 235.

60. Testimony of Warren Buffett, 236.

would be out there trying to get our business, and they would try by price, but they might also try by laxity. You can argue that if there was just one rating agency, they would have no reason to compete on either price or laxity. I mean, independence can really come with—with strength in the business. Ben Franklin said it's difficult for an empty sack to stand straight. So if you really had a situation where there was a lot of competition, I'm not sure that the rating agencies would be as independent actually in coming to their credit conclusions as they are.[61]

The afternoon session of the commission's hearings in New York was scheduled to be headlined by Brian M. Clarkson's testimony. Clarkson, a former president of Moody's Investors Service (August 2007–August 2008), submitted a written statement but was unable to attend the hearing for medical reasons. He has never appeared at a hearing or investigation into the financial crisis and his work at Moody's. Before his rise at Moody's the company was a minor player in rating structured finance, rating only 14 percent of deals before he took over in 1999. This grew to 94 percent (worth $190 billion) in 2007.[62] The structured finance group at Moody's accounted for 43 percent of Moody's revenue in 2006, an increase from 28 percent in 1998. In 2006 the firm made more from structured finance alone—$881 million—than total revenue in 2001.

In his written testimony Clarkson suggested that a confluence of factors was responsible for the crisis. These included historically low interest rates, government policies promoting home ownership, "a sudden and severe nationwide decline in home prices," and a

61. Testimony of Warren Buffett, 290–291.

62. Aaron Lucchetti, "As Housing Boomed, Moody's Opened Up," *Wall Street Journal*, April 11, 2008, https://www.wsj.com/articles/SB120787287341306591, accessed December 30, 2018.

similarly severe, unprecedented shrinkage in refinancing credit.[63] He went on to suggest that Moody's was aware of deteriorating conditions in the housing market and took action between 2003 and 2006 by, among other things, increasing credit protection in securitized deals by about 30 percent. The problem, he suggested, was that the US housing market deteriorated "beyond anyone's expectations," and Moody's, "like many others, did not anticipate the magnitude or severity of the downturn."[64] Clarkson maintained that in structured finance the role of rating agencies remains that of an opinion provider, there to "alleviate some of the information asymmetry" between issuers and investors.[65] He went on to state: "I have been asked whether I believe there is a conflict between the goals of growing market coverage and maintaining ratings quality. I do not. These goals are fundamentally intertwined."[66] He went on to explain this view, predicated on, among other things, the idea that broad coverage allows for greater comparability between issues.[67]

Two former employees of Clarkson's at Moody's testified that day: Mark Froeba and Richard Michalek. Both were lawyers, and Michalek had testified to Senator Levin's subcommittee in April. Froeba says that before Moody's was independently traded on the NYSE in 2000, it had "an extremely conservative analytical culture," and "analysts were proud to work for what they believed was by far

63. Testimony of Brian M. Clarkson, *Financial Crisis Inquiry Commission*, Hearing on "Credibility of Credit Ratings, the Investment Decisions Made Based on Those Ratings, and the Financial Crisis," June 2, 2010, http://fcic-static.law.stanford.edu/cdn_media/fcic-testimony/2010-0602-Clarkson.pdf, accessed December 30, 2018, 1.

64. Testimony of Brian M. Clarkson, 1.

65. Testimony of Brian M. Clarkson, 3.

66. Testimony of Brian M. Clarkson, 3.

67. Testimony of Brian M. Clarkson, 3–4.

the best of the rating agencies."[68] He suggests that Moody's could have stopped the housing bubble, but by the time the housing bubble actually arrived "Moody's had deliberately abandoned its stature, surrendered its power and given up its analytical distinctiveness."[69] Market share was the obsession. In Froeba's words,

> Brian Clarkson quadrupled Moody's market share in the residential mortgage securities group by simply firing or transferring nearly all the analysts in the group and replacing them with analysts willing to apply a new rating methodology. As I am quoted saying about this new approach to the bottom line at Moody's in *The Wall Street Journal* article, there was never an explicit directive to subordinate rating quality to market share; there was, rather, a palpable erosion of institutional support for any rating analysis that threatened market share.[70]

Practically, said Froeba, this meant that "Moody's senior managers never set out to make sure that Moody's rating answers were always wrong. Instead, they put in place a new culture that would not tolerate for long any answer that hurt Moody's bottom line."[71] Froeba, pressed for time by Angelides, skips over the "ways in which Brian [Clarkson] used threats of employment termination to intimidate analysts."[72] He then makes the point that on the "topic of termination . . . as a tool to implement the culture change at Moody's . . . Brian was not a rogue manager running amok."[73]

---

68. Testimony of Mark Froeba, *Financial Crisis Inquiry Commission*, Official Transcript, 345, 346.

69. Testimony of Mark Froeba, 346.

70. Testimony of Mark Froeba, 347–348. The *Wall Street Journal* article referred to by Mr. Froeba is Lucchetti, "As Housing Boomed, Moody's Opened Up."

71. Testimony of Mark Froeba, 348.

72. Testimony of Mark Froeba, 352.

73. Testimony of Mark Froeba, 353.

Richard Michalek confirmed the change in culture identified by Froeba. He experienced a "steady drive towards commoditization of the instruments we were rating."[74] The problem was that this process was not sensitive to "the increasing complexity of the products we were being asked to rate."[75]

WHEN PEOPLE THINK of financial innovation, they inevitably think of computers and highly educated "rocket scientists" developing quantitative techniques for managing risk. But that is not at the heart of this matter. Lawyers are the key to the problem. The real essence of structured finance is to be found in the legal rights to revenues organized in the contracts and trusts that underpin the securities. This documentation can run to thousands of pages. These legal underpinnings give different rights to different tranches of a security. Some, such as the AAA tranche, have the right to be paid first, while others have to wait in line. This is how a mass of not very creditworthy subprime mortgages could produce some AAA bonds. The AAA investors had first right to revenue, and the expectation was that even if some subprime mortgage holders defaulted as expected, enough would pay so that those with the highly rated securities would be paid in full. Unfortunately, when expectations are not met and people are full of uncertainty, as in 2007–2009, this model stopped working. When recession is added to the mix, the result is a wholesale write-down of the global market in securities.[76]

---

74. Testimony of Richard Michalek, *Financial Crisis Inquiry Commission*, Official Transcript, 361.

75. Testimony of Richard Michalek, 361.

76. On the structural foundations of the social dynamics of the recession, see Andrew Gamble, *Crisis without End? The Unravelling of Western Prosperity* (Basingstoke, UK: Palgrave Macmillan, 2014).

As disastrous as this situation was, the rating agencies' real failure was something else, namely, their own move into the markets. For decades Moody's and S&P had played the role of a judge or referee, standing back from the action and making calls as necessary. They were valued for this role, which allowed them to build up substantial reputational assets. But structured finance is only possible with the active involvement of the rating agencies in designing the financial instruments. The agencies and their ratings created the distinct tranches or levels of specific structured finance issues. Some of these tranches were rated AAA. Others were rated lower. Because of the complexity of the legal documentation and protection necessary for these tranches, the raters did not stand back as neutral judges as they normally had. In structured finance, the raters acted more like consultants, helping to construct the securities themselves, indicating how they would rate them if they were organized in ways that offered specific legal protection to investors. This is how the raters imperiled their franchise.

As much as possible I have sought to let the raters and those who questioned them speak for themselves in this chapter. Superficially, this story can perhaps be read as a tale of greed like so many others. But when you think about the authoritative position of the rating agencies, the ideas collectively shared about the veracity of their ratings in the financial community and among the wider public, and the fact that the work of the agencies and their standing as judges of creditworthiness had become constitutive rules of the whole financial system, it is clear that a social foundations approach is necessary to appreciate the dynamics of these events.

In the next chapter I will examine the rise of the agencies from calamity and how it became clear they were as relevant as ever.

6

Aftermath

It was dumb enough to create a system that
encourages the credit rating agencies to take a
Panglossian view of the bonds they're supposedly
rating. It'd be even dumber to leave it in place after
we've seen what a disaster it is.

—*Matt O'Brien,* Washington Post

The credit-rating agencies, legislative handwaving
aside, were able to escape significant regulation and
reform.

—*Barry Eichengreen,*
Hall of Mirrors, *2015*

The key problem is that . . . bold actions aimed at
the substance of CRAs' [credit rating agencies'] and
firms' risk assessment approaches . . . might be a
cure worse than the disease . . . regulators fear that
sweeping reforms will either reinforce ratings'
systemic effects, or that they will merely shift these
destabilizing consequences from one set of risk
indicators to another.

—*Bart Stellinga, "Why Performativity Limits Credit
Rating Reform," 2019*

> CRAs play a vital role in pricing that which has no
> definite price—the riskiness of assets in a future
> that has yet to be realized and that cannot be
> reduced to its time series past. . . . CRAs, like
> democracy, may be the worst system of all, apart
> from all the other alternatives.
>
> —*Rawi Abdelal and Mark Blyth,*
> *"Just Who Put You in Charge?," 2015*

This chapter is about the survival of the agencies. The agencies failed, but unlike auditor Arthur Andersen, they did not die. Moody's, S&P, and Fitch remain key institutions in the capital markets and are highly profitable. How did these institutions that have been accused of terrible wrongdoing, incompetence, and corruption, carry on, and what marks out this persistence from the institutions that did not survive? The central question about the survival of the agencies is whether their continued existence is a matter of good fortune, because they happen to be in a strategic position and thus necessary, or whether their survival has been orchestrated by the agencies themselves. Other things equal, if survival is the good luck of the agencies to be essential in specific circumstances, with the passage of time, the rise of new institutions and new circumstances should bring change. If the agencies' hand in their own survival is more active, they may have a brighter future.

I offer a two-pronged explanation for the persistence of the agencies. Rating agencies purport to solve an information problem in disintermediated capital markets. We do not at present have institutions that do this job better than the rating agencies, despite whatever failings we attribute to them. Homeostasis, or the persistence of an existing system in the absence of compelling reasons for change, can explain their persistence.

The other dimension to survival of the agencies is the continuing dominance of the Big Three. The top agencies, Moody's, S&P, and Fitch, have not given way to the many smaller, less prominent agencies in the years since the crisis began, despite blame being directed toward the Big Three and efforts to open the rating market by authorities in the United States and Europe. Nor has transparency made any significant difference.

I argue that the continued dominance of the Big Three reflects the reality that some judgments have more weight than others in the capital markets. This bias to a small set of long-established rating agencies is constitutive of the rating system. Not all judgments are equal. Concentration of market share in a few hands is not a matter of chance. Concentration reflects what ratings provide to those who use them. In ratings, reputation is exclusive; it favors incumbents and is a major barrier to start-ups, regardless of government efforts to liberalize the market for ratings.[1] Failing to recognize this hierarchy of epistemic authority in rating has been a significant error in the efforts to reform credit rating policy since the Enron failure. It reflects the dominance of a market-centered approach to thinking about the rating agencies, which cannot explain their power and persistence.

Shared Assumptions

After the crisis there was a debate about what to do about agency regulation. I discussed regulation of the agencies in chapter 2, and I examine some of the key issues in the postcrisis debate further toward the end of this chapter. Given how much vitriol was directed

---

1. Mennillo and Sinclair, "A Hard Nut to Crack," 270.

toward the agencies during the crisis and in the years that followed, it would be reasonable to assume that this debate involved different political interests, competing regulatory bodies, and politicians facing off against each other, as on so many other issues. But that expectation is a mistake. I do not see evidence of the issues being treated in this way. Aside from the agencies going "on strike" over Section 939G in Dodd-Frank, which led to the revocation of that provision in 2011 via the Asset-Backed Market Stabilization Act, as documented in chapter 2, the debate about regulating or reregulating agencies does not take a combative form. The reason the debate takes mostly the form of a civil discussion is down to two things. The first, and less interesting, is that the agencies do what seems technical work that few people understand. This excludes most from the debate, and aside from rhetoric, makes it hard for those unwilling to focus on the detail to really come to grips with the issues. The second thing that explains this remarkably low-key debate about agency reregulation is the preexisting mental framework about rating, which I have argued in previous work conditions our thinking about what rating is and what it can become.[2] Because participants to the regulatory debate share this mental framework of rating orthodoxy, they are able to have a remarkably civil debate about rating, within the narrow limits of those assumptions. As we will see in the second half of this chapter, sharing assumptions about what rating is and should be does not resolve the rating enigma.

Organizing the Markets

On July 27, 2011, a hearing into oversight of the credit rating agencies after Dodd-Frank was held by the US House of Represen-

---

2. Sinclair, *The New Masters of Capital*, 69–70.

tatives' Subcommittee on Oversight and Investigations.[3] Representative Randy Neugebauer, chairman of the subcommittee, began the session by noting how concentrated the rating industry remains after the global financial crisis and Dodd-Frank, with 98 percent of ratings and 90 percent of revenue in the hands of Moody's, S&P, and Fitch.[4] He noted in his opening remarks that the agencies are "a very important part of our economy. A lot of people still put a lot of credence into these ratings" despite their role in the global financial crisis. It was, he suggested, "extremely important" to restore "more certainty" to this market. Neugebauer was followed by Representative Michael E. Capuano, who suggested that the agencies have "finally done what we had all hoped and wanted them to do." He asserted that they are now more reliable, more independent, and have "changed their model significantly."[5] Representative Spencer Bachus, chairman of the Financial Services Committee, noted how Section 939A of Dodd-Frank sought to reduce the role of rating agencies by removing ratings from federal statutes and rules. But other sections of the law, such as Section 939F, reinforced the role of rating agencies by potentially requiring the SEC to create a system for choosing the rating agency for an issuer's structured finance instruments.[6] He went on to note how rules adopted by the SEC in May 2011, mandated by the 2006 Credit Rating Agency Reform Act, to open up NRSRO designation to

---

3. "Oversight of the Credit Rating Agencies Post-Dodd-Frank," Subcommittee on Oversight and Investigations of the Committee on Financial Services, US House of Representatives, July 27, 2011, https://www.govinfo.gov/content/pkg/CHRG-112hhrg67946/pdf/CHRG-112hhrg67946.pdf, accessed August 28, 2019.

4. Neugebauer, "Oversight of the Credit Rating Agencies," 2.

5. Capuano, "Oversight of the Credit Rating Agencies," 3.

6. A system never implemented.

new applicants, erected "life-threatening" new barriers to entry to rating start-ups.[7]

Much of the evidence from witnesses at this hearing concerned the challenge of replacing credit ratings with alternative specifications of creditworthiness that were as granular, or as specific, as ratings.[8] But removing ratings from rules did not mean removing ratings from the market, because the market would still demand them. Mr. Capuano, the ranking member from Massachusetts, questioned David K. Wilson, senior deputy comptroller, Office of the Comptroller of the Currency:

> *Mr. Capuano*: Is there anything in any rule anywhere that prohibits the market from looking at a credit rating from anybody?
>
> *Mr. Wilson*: No.
>
> *Mr. Capuano*: So that you can't make them do it, but you can't stop them from doing it either? Is that a fair statement?
>
> *Mr. Wilson*: It has to be removed from the regulations. It doesn't mean that the investor can't—
>
> *Mr. Capuano*: That is what I am suggesting. The market is going to call for a credit rating no matter what we do. I think it is a good thing to get them out. I think it is a good thing to do. But I don't want to pretend that is going to be the end of all our troubles. The market is still going to be looking for a credit rating. Do you think that is a fair statement? Does anybody think it is an unfair statement?
>
> *Mr. Van Der Weide*: It seems fair.[9]

---

7. Bachus, "Oversight of the Credit Rating Agencies," 3.

8. "Oversight of the Credit Rating Agencies." See comments at the bottom of page 12 and in the middle of page 23.

9. Bachus, "Oversight of the Credit Rating Agencies," 20.

Later in the hearing, the question of alternatives to rating was discussed between the congressmen and the witnesses, and it seems there were none for now. Homeostasis was the rule:

> *Mr. Canseco*: Do you believe it is good public policy for the government to mandate the use of credit ratings by privately owned companies, then use those ratings as the basis for capital requirements?
>
> *Mr. Wilson*: It is one of those [situations] where it is the best option we have. And I think that is what the Basel Committee came to. So it is a hard answer. But until we can find a better option, I think that is at least what the Basel Committee decided.
>
> *Mr. Canseco*: Do you have an opinion, other than the Basel requirement?
>
> *Mr. Wilson*: Yes. I think it is difficult because I don't have another option that is better.
>
> *Mr. Canseco*: Okay.
>
> *Mr. Wilson*: If you want to be risk sensitive.[10]

The second session of the hearing featured testimony from Lawrence J. White, a professor of economics at the Stern School of Business, New York University. White, one of the most acute scholarly observers of the rating agencies, expressed concern about the effects of increased regulation in his opening statement, and advocated repeal of these provisions in Dodd-Frank:

> The advocates of such regulation want figuratively, perhaps literally, to grab the rating agencies by the lapels, shake them, and shout, "Do a better job."
>
> This urge for greater regulation is understandable and well-intentioned, but it is misguided and potentially quite harmful. The

---

10. Bachus, 24.

heightened regulation of the rating agencies is likely to discourage entry, rigidify a specified set of structures and procedures, and discourage innovation in new ways of gathering and assessing information, new technologies, new methodologies, and new models, possibly including new business models, and may well not achieve the goal of inducing better ratings from the agencies.

Ironically, these provisions will also likely create a protective barrier around the larger credit rating agencies and are thus likely to make them even more central to and important for the bond markets of the future.

Why would we want to do that?[11]

The following year, at a hearing on the agencies before the Treasury Select Committee of the House of Commons in London, Georg Grodzki, then head of credit research at Legal & General Investment Management, an investment manager based in England, explained to members of Parliament why his firm still used the outputs of the agencies.[12] He noted that customers vary in their "degree of risk appetite," which is captured in the Investment Management Agreement (IMA) between his firm and customers. Grodzki said his firm had to

make sure we are in compliance [with the IMA], which sometimes can force us to sell securities if they are downgraded below a certain level, or buy them if they are upgraded. Also, even if we are not directly affected, we need to anticipate the market's response

---

11. White, "Oversight of the Credit Rating Agencies," 37. On the dilemmas of regulation, see Anil Hira, Norbert Gaillard, and Theodore H. Cohn, eds., *The Failure of Financial Regulation: Why a Major Crisis Could Happen Again* (Cham, Switzerland: Palgrave Macmillan / Springer Nature Switzerland, 2019).

12. The quotations that follow are from Oral Evidence before the Treasury Committee, "Inquiry into Credit Rating Agencies," House of Commons, February 29, 2012. This is the uncorrected transcript (there is no corrected transcript). Available at https://publications.parliament.uk/pa/cm201012/cmselect/cmtreasy /uc1866-i/uc186601.htm, accessed September 5, 2019 (unpaginated).

due to such rating references. We need to anticipate the market's response to a certain rating action because the market response could mean prices move, and of course we want to be on the right side of the next pricing move and that means we have to look at them [ratings].

This response prompted the committee chair to ask if Grodzki thought the agencies did a better job than Legal & General at the analytical work of rating.

The fact that they are doing a job that is normally in our world, which is corporate credit ratings, reasonably is positive because the market benefits from a diversity of opinions. We use them as a reference point. We use them as a discussion partner, as a source of information, so the market's thinking and reflection of credit quality is enhanced by institutions that regularly produce verdicts on credit quality.

John Grout, of the Association of Corporate Treasurers, explained that the "rating agencies offered a lot of convenience to people in his industry." They also offered a different perspective, "more than just the historical numbers that have been published," because

they are interested in policy strategy and, particularly nowadays, risk management within the company. That is the non-public bit. There may be other things, but that is the non-public bit, which I think is important to the rating agencies. It is not what this year's profit is going to be, which is perhaps what it might be assumed to be, but that is much, much less relevant to a credit analyst than it is to an equity analyst. The kind of conversation that goes on would normally drive an equity analyst potty because it is about how you deal with long-term risk and that sort of thing.

Grout went on to observe that in the 1970s when he managed a fund worth several hundred million pounds, there were no credit ratings in England: "You struggled to get a sensible set of criteria. There were not even the kind of credit analysts that exist today that you could subscribe to. The rating agencies are a huge convenience and for smaller companies than the one I was working for, that convenience is not substitutable by saying, 'Employ more people or pay large fees to other people.' If you are a medium-sized company here in the UK, it is a very useful thing to do."

Grodzki sought to qualify this view by suggesting there is a lot more transparency about corporate performance today when compared to the 1970s, so "the market is less disadvantaged these days, relative to the agencies' privilege [of proprietary information], than it used to be 30 years ago." However, he went on to note that smaller investors would still struggle without ratings today. He also added that for some investors ratings are sufficient for their decision making, because they "decide that is good enough for them, so they still have that naive, or not naive, trust in the ratings. It saves them time." It might be concluded that they do not have a better alternative. Homeostasis makes them stick with what they have.

European Sovereign Debt Crisis

If anyone thought the rating agencies were irrelevant in the wake of the global financial crisis, the European sovereign debt crisis that followed the market meltdown should have put those ideas to rest.[13]

---

13. On sovereign ratings, see Norbert Gaillard, *A Century of Sovereign Ratings* (New York: Springer, 2012), and Norbert Gaillard, *Country Risk: The Bane of Foreign Investors* (New York: Springer, 2020). For a more conceptual account, see Bartholomew Paudyn, *Credit Ratings and Sovereign Debt: The Political Economy of Creditworthiness through Risk and Uncertainty* (London: Palgrave Macmillan, 2014). Also see Marion Fourcade, "State Metrology: The Rating of Sovereigns and the Judgment of Nations," in *The Many Hands of the State: Theorizing Politi-*

My claim is not that ratings have a major, direct impact on sovereign credit in general, or that they were pivotal in the European sovereign debt crisis in particular. Instead, the European sovereign rating crisis shows that ratings are still perceived as important in financial markets, despite a presumed negative reputational impact of the global financial crisis on the agencies.

Zsófia Barta and Alison Johnston provide empirical evidence of partisan-biased sovereign rating downgrades and resulting "partisan discrimination" in sovereign bond markets.[14] The sovereign debt crisis in Europe gave rise to a body of literature that discusses further facets of "sovereign rating failure." Andreas Fuchs and Kai Gehring show how sovereign ratings have suffered from a "home bias" in the aftermath of the global financial crisis that started in 2007.[15] The Big Three gave European states excessively severe sovereign ratings compared to the US sovereign rating. Similarly, Manfred Gärtner and Björn Griesbach suggest that ratings have a nonlinear effect on interest rates, facilitating self-fulfilling prophecy scenarios (or "multiple equilibria") in sovereign debt markets.[16] In another study, Manfred Gärtner, Björn Griesbach, and Florian Jung (2011) find that economic fundamentals cannot explain

cal Authority and Social Control, ed. Kimberly J. Morgan and Ann Shola Orloff (New York: Cambridge University Press, 2017).

14. Z. Barta and A. Johnston, "Rating Politics? Partisan Discrimination in Credit Ratings in Developed Economies," *Comparative Political Studies* 51, no. 5 (2018): 587–620. This paragraph is based on Mennillo and Sinclair, "A Hard Nut to Crack."

15. A. Fuchs and K. Gehring, "The Home Bias in Sovereign Ratings," *Journal of the European Economic Association* 15, no. 6 (2017): 1386–1423.

16. M. Gärtner and B. Griesbach, "Rating Agencies, Self-Fulfilling Prophecy and Multiple Equilibria? An Empirical Model of the European Sovereign Debt Crisis, 2009–2011," Economics Working Paper Series, No. 1215 (University of St. Gallen, School of Economics and Political Science, 2012).

sovereign ratings during the European sovereign debt crisis.[17] Variation differs both in the past and across countries.

The deterioration in government finances that followed the acute phase of the global financial crisis affected most states in Europe, but hit Portugal, Ireland, Italy, Greece, and Spain (known at the time as the PIIGS) especially hard. The response to the burden of the bailouts and falling tax revenues was austerity programs to cut government spending across the EU.[18] Tooze shows how European banks were heavily involved in structured finance before the crisis and that the Federal Reserve worked "hand in glove" with these institutions to unwind their positions after 2008.[19] This "dramatic reassertion of the pivotal role of America's central bank" massively increased the centrality of the dollar as European conditions deteriorated.[20]

If a collapse of market confidence was key to the evaporation of liquidity between 2007 and 2009, leading to Germain's "great freeze" in capital markets, confidence was again the issue after the acute phase of the crisis, but now confidence was focused on fiscal problems.[21] Banks in northern Europe were heavily involved in lending to financial institutions in the PIIGS, making this a crisis for the eurozone as a whole. Tooze identifies a three-tiered struc-

---

17. M. Gärtner, B. Griesbach, and F. Jung, "PIGS or Lambs? The European Sovereign Debt Crisis and the Role of Rating Agencies," *International Advances in Economic Research* 17, no. 3 (2011): 288–299.

18. On austerity as a response to the crisis, see Mark Blyth, *Austerity: The History of a Dangerous Idea* (New York: Oxford University Press, 2013), especially chap. 3. On austerity and urban politics, especially in Detroit, see Sarah Phinney, "Detroit's Municipal Bankruptcy: Racialised Geographies of Austerity," *New Political Economy* 23, no. 5 (2018): 609–626. Also see Tooze, *Crashed*, 287.

19. Tooze, 210.

20. Tooze, 219.

21. On this great freeze, see Randall Germain, *Global Politics and Financial Governance* (London: Palgrave Macmillan, 2010), 79; for fiscal problems, see Tooze, 290.

ture, with the small insolvent states of Greece and Portugal at the bottom, then states that had to pick up the costs of the real estate boom (and bust)—Spain and Ireland—and then Italy, the big debtor at the top. Greece and what happened to it were less important than "holding this giant pyramid in place." Abdelal and Blyth suggest that the ratings of these states gave Germany—even though the German banks had lent prodigiously—"advocacy tools to beat the Spanish sovereign into austerity and reform and to keep the Greeks in the Euro at all costs."[22] As they see it, ratings mattered in the euro sovereign debt crisis because they were key to "codifying the conventional judgement as to what 'average opinion ought to be,' as Keynes put it many years ago."[23] Tooze labels the European strategy for this early period of the sovereign debt crisis "extend-and-pretend."[24]

This "extend-and-pretend" system came unstuck when Fitch downgraded Greek government debt in April 2010, leading to yields surging to 7.4 percent. After this, interbank lending between European banks was massively curtailed, creating circumstances similar to those of late 2008 in the repo markets.[25] Tooze discusses at some length how German domestic politics, among other things, led to this situation in which Greek problems threatened international spillover.[26] S&P downgraded Greece to junk bond status in June 2010, raising the question of whether the eurozone could handle the bigger problems in Spain and Italy.[27] By September 2011, the three countries judged the most likely to default—Greece, Ireland,

22. Abdelal and Blyth, "Just Who Put You in Charge?," 53.
23. Abdelal and Blyth, 53.
24. Tooze, *Crashed*, 328.
25. Tooze, 339.
26. Tooze, 345.
27. Tooze, 385.

and Portugal—were all in the eurozone. They were thought to be in worse shape than Belarus, Venezuela, and Pakistan.[28] It emerged that institutional investors, including banks, had to dump these bonds as their ratings fell, adding to mounting concerns and helping to dry up wholesale funding.[29] From the middle of 2011, proposals appeared in Europe to censor or otherwise restrain the agencies from undertaking sovereign ratings.[30] Eventually, the European Parliament and the Council created some rules about publication dates for sovereign ratings.[31] Lucia Quaglia notes that the downgrades by US-headquartered rating agencies "gave new momentum to the debate on the creation of the European rating agency" within the European Parliament.[32]

Things came to a head, systemically speaking, in 2012. S&P downgraded Portugal to "junk" standing in January, as well as downgrading France and Austria, who both lost their AAA ratings.[33] But it was the problems in Spain that moved the response in the eurozone on from "extend-and-pretend." In June 2012, Moody's downgraded Spain to Baa3, just one notch above junk or speculative status. Spain was "clearly sliding toward the abyss." It

---

28. Tooze, 387.

29. Tooze, 387.

30. Ian Traynor, "EU Declares War on Agencies as Ireland's Rating Gets Junk Status," *The Guardian*, July 13, 2011, https://www.theguardian.com/business/2011/jul/12/eu-war-on-credit-ratings-agencies, accessed July 13, 2011. Holman W. Jenkins Jr., "Who Elected the Rating Agencies?," *Wall Street Journal*, July 27, 2011. "The Road to Self-Deception," *The Economist*, November 12, 2011, 83. Also see Nicolas Véron, *Rate Expectations: What Can and Cannot Be Done about Rating Agencies*, Bruegel Policy Contribution, Issue 2011/14, October 2011.

31. Regulation (EU) No. 462/2013 of the European Parliament and of the Council of 21 May 2013 amending Regulation (EC) No. 1060/2009 on credit rating agencies. See clause 40.

32. Quaglia, "Regulatory Response of the European Union," 181. No such agency was created.

33. Tooze, *Crashed*, 421.

was at this point that the banking union was agreed in the EU, establishing collective responsibility for the continent's financial institutions.[34] At the end of the following month, Mario Draghi, president of the European Central Bank (ECB), made a speech in London in which he asserted that the ECB was ready to do "whatever it takes to preserve the euro."[35] Subsequently, the ECB formalized its new role as lender of last resort, although heavily qualified, as Outright Monetary Transactions.[36] With this change the ECB became much more like the Federal Reserve, and the markets stabilized.[37] Interestingly for our story, the ECB integrated credit ratings into the qualifications for inclusion in its quantitative easing program, despite government concerns that the agencies were "reckless" in their rating of European states.[38]

S&P Downgrades the USA

For much of the last century the creditworthiness of the US government and the US sovereign credit rating have been unsurpassed, functioning as a haven for capital when market and political volatility erupted elsewhere. As Paul Langley noted, now, even for the United States, "the spectre of a bond rating downgrade loomed large. This was assumed to automatically result in an increase in the interest that investors would demand in return for holding government debt, and therefore lead to a worsening of deficits and debt."[39]

---

34. Tooze, 436. S&P downgraded Spain in October 2012.
35. Draghi, quoted in Tooze, 438.
36. Tooze, 441.
37. Tooze, 444.
38. Tooze, 536; Paudyn, *Credit Ratings and Sovereign Debt*, 3.
39. Paul Langley, *Liquidity Lost: The Governance of the Global Financial Crisis* (Oxford: Oxford University Press, 2015), 158.

So, it was a shock when S&P downgraded the US sovereign rating from AAA to AA+ in August 2011.[40] Tooze mentions the "'political brinksmanship'" cited by S&P in its explanation of the downgrade.[41] Bartholomew Paudyn sees this downgrade as a moment in the struggle between what he calls epistocracy—"knowledge-based expert rule"—and democracy.[42] Daniel Drezner sees it as a clear win for the US government and economy, because the downgrade did not stop the purchase of US government securities.[43] The downgrade was controversial. Bernanke suggests that the "episode highlighted the odd relationship between governments and rating agencies: Governments regulate the rating agencies, but the rating agencies have the power to downgrade governments' debt."[44] Allegations and rumors about the downgrade and actions by the US government continued for years.[45] The downgrade was followed by a dispute about how the rating was determined, in which S&P was accused of making a $2 trillion mistake.[46] S&P defended its work in the House of Commons in London on April 24,

40. Paudyn, *Credit Ratings and Sovereign Debt*, 3.

41. Tooze, *Crashed*, 392.

42. Paudyn, *Credit Ratings and Sovereign Debt*, 2.

43. Daniel Drezner, *The System Worked: How the World Stopped Another Great Depression* (New York: Oxford University Press, 2014), 125.

44. Ben S. Bernanke, *The Courage to Act: A Memoir of a Crisis and its Aftermath* (New York: Norton, 2015), 511. Bernanke's comment implies more meaningful regulation of the agencies than has ever existed.

45. Bradley Hope and Damian Paletta, "S&P Chief Says Geithner Warned about U.S. Downgrade: Treasury Secretary Allegedly Said Firm Would Be Held Accountable," *Wall Street Journal*, January 21, 2014, https://www.wsj.com/articles/geithner-warned-sampp-about-us-downgrade-legal-filing-1390323921, accessed October 8, 2019.

46. On former US Treasury secretary Geithner's view of the "mistake," see Timothy F. Geithner, *Stress Test: Reflections on Financial Crises* (New York: Random House, 2014), 471–472.

2012.[47] Under intense questioning about whether there was an error, Moritz Kraemer for S&P said:

> No, there was no mistake made by either side. They are different scenarios. These are measures about the future. You have to have an analytical debate on what is the likely strategy of fiscal consolidation the Government might take. These are all CBO [Congressional Budget Office] scenarios that we use. This is not an S&P scenario. The question was merely, which of the various CBO scenarios that have been published should be underlying the rating assessment. Now, we did agree with the Treasury that it should be the baseline scenario, which would lead to $20 [tr]illion rather than $22 [tr]illion. So there was no mistake on their side and there was no mistake on our side.

The House of Commons committee were curious about the fall in yields on US Treasury bonds since the downgrade and asked Kraemer to explain this paradox, which he did by invoking an investor flight to quality and suggesting that the new downgraded US rating still implied "an extremely small probability of default."

Another member of the committee suggested the US downgrade revealed the agencies flexing their muscles:

> *Andrea Leadsom:* Mr Riley, do you think that it is reasonable for a ratings agency to effectively hold a Government to ransom, saying unless they do something about their debt ceiling then they will lose their AAA status? Is that a reasonable way for a credit rating agency to behave?

---

47. The quotations that follow are from Oral Evidence before the Treasury Committee, "Inquiry into Credit Rating Agencies," House of Commons, April 24, 2012. This is the uncorrected transcript (there is no corrected transcript). Available at https://publications.parliament.uk/pa/cm201012/cmselect/cmtreasy/uc1866-iii /uc186601.htm, accessed September 5, 2019 (unpaginated). Billion has been changed to trillion to correct error.

David Riley: I do not think it is reasonable for a credit rating agency to, as you suggest, hold a Government to ransom. I think it is reasonable for a credit rating agency to express an opinion as to what might influence the credit rating and if that is a failure to reach agreement on raising the debt ceiling, which could result potentially in a missed payment on a debt security, it would be remiss, frankly, of a rating agency not to express an opinion as to the likelihood of such an event and what that might imply.

Andrea Leadsom: To what extent should ratings agencies take into account the public nature of sovereign debt ratings at such a very sensitive time in the immediate aftermath of a global financial crisis? What kind of public duty do they have to try and preserve credibility in sovereigns?

David Riley: I think it is incumbent upon all of us, including the rating agencies, to do the role that we play in terms of each of the participants within the market . . . not by pretending those issues are not there but to try to address them in terms of our ratings in a very timely but also in a very transparent manner.

Competition

The other dimension of the survival of the agencies is the continued dominance of the Big Three as opposed to other agencies. The top agencies, Moody's, S&P, and Fitch, have not given way to the many smaller, less prominent agencies in the years since the crisis began.[48] I argue that the continued dominance of the Big Three reflects the reality that some judgments are more important than others in the capital markets. This focus on the long-established rating agencies is, it seems, a constitutive feature of the rating system. Concentration is not a matter of chance. It reflects the discrimina-

---

48. This section and the next are based on Mennillo and Sinclair, "A Hard Nut to Crack," 269–275.

tion users of ratings want. Reputation is not egalitarian and open to all comers who provide the service. It is exclusive and a zero-sum game. This favors incumbents and is a major barrier to start-ups. Government efforts to liberalize the market have not changed this dynamic. These efforts have failed because they are not based on a social foundations approach to rating. Failing to recognize the hierarchy of epistemic authority in rating has undermined efforts to reform credit rating policy.

Conventional accounts read the credit rating agencies' success story as a result of weak competition. The idea that the enhancement of competition can reduce the flaws in the rating industry and promote rating "objectivity" is not new. In the United States, it goes back at least to the Credit Rating Agency Reform Act of 2006. In the EU, the "promotion of competition and more market players on the credit rating market" is part of the post–global financial crisis regulations.[49] The scholarly literature has not tired of recommending "a competitive environment" as the "means to achieve better credit ratings."[50] In mainstream economic thinking, the main purpose of regulation is "to constrain the use of monopoly power and the prevention of serious distortions to competition."[51] On this logic, in rating, weak competition leads to poor analysis as the credit rating agencies lack incentives to reinvest in their product. From this perspective,

49. European Commission, "New Rules on Credit Rating Agencies (CRAs) Enter into Force—Frequently Asked Questions," 2013, http://europa.eu/rapid/press-release_MEMO-13-571_en.htm, accessed March 21, 2018.

50. A. Darbellay, *Regulating Credit Rating Agencies* (Cheltenham: Edward Elgar, 2013); F. Amtenbrink and K. Heine, "Regulating Credit Rating Agencies in the European Union: Lessons from Behavioural Science," *Dovenschmidt Quarterly* 2, no. 1 (2013): 2–15.

51. M. Brunnermeier et al., *The Fundamental Principles of Financial Regulation*, Geneva Reports on the World Economy, International Center for Monetary and Banking Studies, 2009.

regulatory measures should increase the degree of competition to bring about a "better" market outcome in the form of more accurate ratings.

Striving for a level playing field and reducing entry barriers for smaller market players will not automatically diminish the probability of rating failure and improve rating quality. The global rating market consists of more than eighty players, but the Big Three still hold more than 90 percent of market share.[52] This suggests a stable equilibrium between smaller market players and the Big Three. The former either operate locally or are specialized in niche markets and specific sectors.[53] Building strategic alliances or bandwagoning with the Big Three benefits small agencies in terms of reputation, publicity, and credibility. The largest credit rating agencies can reinforce their dominant global market position. This "win-win situation" reinforces homeostasis in the rating market.

Rating is highly concentrated, both overall and at the individual product category level, including corporate bonds and sovereign bonds, and in structured finance.[54] There exists a *general preference toward large credit rating agencies* and a *shared view among investors (and also issuers) that small credit rating agencies provide lower quality ratings compared to large credit rating agencies.* Against this background, it is not surprising that regulations aimed at promoting competition and increasing the number of smaller market players

---

52. G. Mattarocci, *The Independence of Credit Rating Agencies: How Business Models and Regulators Interact* (Oxford: Elsevier Academic Press, 2014), 121.

53. J. G. Coffee Jr., "Ratings Reform: The Good, the Bad, and the Ugly," *Harvard Business Law Review* 1 (2011): 231–278. Also see J. G. Coffee Jr., *Gatekeepers: The Professions and Corporate Governance* (New York: Oxford University Press, 2006), chap. 8.

54. European Commission, *Study on the State of the Credit Rating Market Final Report—Executive Summary*, 2016, 5, https://ec.europa.eu/info/system/files/state-of -credit-rating-market-study-01012016_en.pdf, accessed March 21, 2018.

have not been effective. Instead, the Big Three oligopoly seems to be a constitutive feature of the rating market.

A rating provides a *centralized* judgment about creditworthiness. By definition, this function can only be fulfilled with a limited number of rating suppliers. With an infinite number of suppliers, the centralized and discriminating raison d'être of rating would evaporate. Therefore, reputational entry barriers are not only the cause for the low degree of competition, but a necessary feature of how rating has worked for the past century. Concentration of market share is the consequence.

One lesson to draw from this is that fostering competition will not automatically lead to the desired ends. We know, after all, that the rise of Fitch into the Big Three did not make rating more competitive after the start of the new millennium. Regulators must acknowledge the constitutive character of the reputational entry barriers, which cannot simply be regulated out of existence. Related to this, they should beware of equating these barriers with a presumptive track record of the incumbent oligopoly. Reputation is inherently exclusive and not necessarily meritocratic and sensitive to performance. It favors the status quo. Therefore, the idea that smaller agencies can catch up with the Big Three by developing a good track record may be wrong.[55]

Transparency

The effort to create competition in rating failed, helping perpetuate the Big Three agencies that had all the advantages. The other side of this orthodox market-centered misunderstanding of rating

---

55. European Commission, *Study on the State of the Credit Rating Market Final Report*, 8.

is transparency. Promoting this failed too, for similar reasons. What O. Kessler describes as the "transparency discourse," which can be traced back at least to the Asian financial crisis of the late 1990s, continued into the realm of rating agency regulation.[56] "Higher transparency" became one of the dominant themes, if not *the* dominant theme, of credit rating agency regulation. The idea that transparency could cure the flaws of the rating industry is a recipe to be found, for example, in the first version of the IOSCO Code and the Credit Rating Agency Reform Act of 2006.[57] The perception that there is a fundamental transparency deficit in the industry in need of repair is widely shared among regulators, policymakers, and scholars alike. Given this, the agencies themselves, independently of regulations imposed, put new transparency measures in place in response to the financial crisis. Embracing transparency—a kind of virtue signaling—has allowed the agencies to demonstrate their ability and willingness to learn from mistakes.

Let us look at some areas suffering from a presumed transparency deficit, what was done about it, and what difference it made. The Credit Rating Agency Reform Act of 2006 put an end to the established but uncodified NRSRO system, establishing criteria for NRSRO recognition for the first time.[58] In the aftermath of the cri-

---

56. O. Kessler, "The Failure of Failure: On Constructivism, the Limits of Critique, and the Socio-political Economy of Economics," *Millennium: Journal of International Studies* 44, no. 3 (2016): 348–369. Also see O. Kessler, "Towards an Economic Sociology of the Subprime Crisis," *Economic Sociology_The European Electronic Newsletter* 10, no. 2 (March 2009): 11–16, http://econsoc.mpifg.de /archive/econ_soc_10-2.pdf, accessed October 22, 2019.

57. International Organisation of Securities Commissions, *Code of Conduct Fundamentals for Credit Rating Agencies*, 2004, 3, http://www.iosco.org/library /pubdocs/pdf/IOSCOPD180.pdf, accessed March 21, 2018.

58. C. Brummer and R. Loko, "The New Politics of Transatlantic Credit Rating Agency Regulation," in *Transnational Financial Regulation after the Crisis*, ed. T. Porter (London: Routledge, 2014), 160. Also see C. Brummer, *Soft Law and the*

sis, the United States formalized registration to facilitate market access for new NRSRO candidates. It has concurrently enhanced disclosure requirements for the registration process as a quality-safeguarding mechanism.[59] The EU introduced a registration duty for credit rating agencies at the same time. Before the financial crisis, European countries de facto adopted the recognition model from the US SEC without defining formal procedures of their own. This "free-riding on American regulatory efforts" was facilitated by the fact that the largest agencies were headquartered in the United States.[60]

The rating failures of the past did not happen because of a "shadow" credit rating industry operating off the regulatory radar. The Big Three were anything but unknown or unacknowledged players. Against this backdrop, it seems unlikely that institutionalized registration and recognition procedures are effective tools to prevent a future rating fiasco. Even though some additional agencies have become NRSROs under the new rules, none of them have any appreciable market share compared to the Big Three.

On conflicts of interest, new regulations aim to mitigate the distorting impact of conflicts of interest on rating quality. Given that eliminating conflicts of interest is out of reach given the current business model, enhanced "disclosure" requirements are treated as an alternative means to address the issue. While the EU adopts a more general approach, the United States requires detailed descriptions

---

Global Financial System: Rule-Making in the 21st Century (New York: Cambridge University Press, 2012), 210–265; T. J. Sinclair, "Global Financial Crises," in *Issues in 21st Century World Politics*, 2nd ed., ed. M. Beeson and N. Bisley (London: Palgrave Macmillan, 2013), 88.

59. S. Hiss and S. Nagel, "Credit Rating Agencies," in *Europe and the Governance of Global Finance*, ed. D. Mügge (Oxford: Oxford University Press, 2014), 140.

60. Sinclair, "Global Financial Crises," 88.

depending on the type of conflicts of interest. As these transparency and disclosure measures mainly affect the conflicts of interest at the individual analyst level, critics have been quick to point out that structural conflicts of interest continue to exist. The new transparency requirements are "a distraction from the principal conflict of interest that distorts ratings, namely, the NRSROs' imperative to maximize revenues and earnings."[61] Indeed, the European Commission maintains that "none of the requirements related to conflicts of interest affected [credit rating agencies and issuers] in a significant way, and as such they cannot be described as either positive or negative." Based on market participants' views, there is little evidence "to draw any firm conclusions on the effectiveness of the disclosure provision" borne by issuers.[62]

Why should enhanced transparency make a difference? Rendering conflicts of interest more transparent does not mean they cease to exist. Conflicts of interest in the industry were no secret in the years preceding the crisis. The attempt to boost rating quality by making conflicts of interest more transparent reveals a certain understanding of rating failure. Rating failure is constructed as the inevitable consequence of the rent-seeking behavior of rational, profit-maximizing firms. It is taken for granted that credit rating agencies want to please issuers more than investors, resulting in less severe ratings. Conflicts of interest and their consequences are thus accepted as given. Increased transparency is therefore not supposed to erase but to mitigate the distorting effects of conflicts of interest on the quality of ratings. The underlying logic is that the public eye

---

61. N. J. Gaillard and W. J. Harrington, "Efficient, Commonsense Actions to Foster Accurate Credit Ratings," *Capital Markets Law Journal* 11, no. 1 (2016): 52.

62. European Commission, *Study on the State of the Credit Rating Market Final Report—Executive Summary*, 9.

has a disciplining effect on rating agencies' "natural" behavior of profit maximization.

This view can be harmful, however, when it silences other causes of rating failure that go beyond the rational-choice approach. For example, credit rating agencies issue unsolicited sovereign ratings without being paid by the bond issuers, and rating failure happens anyway. Regulators should therefore refrain from perceiving every problem of rating as a problem of incentives and conflicts of interest. Transparency is not a magic bullet.

Increasing the transparency of rating methodology in order to make rating actions traceable has also been a popular reform measure after the global financial crisis, as can be seen in the revised IOSCO Code[63] or in EU legislation.[64] Proponents of such "process-based" approaches emphasize the importance of opening up the black box of rating to increase rating quality and prevent rating failure. For example, Kiff, Nowak, and Schumacher call for "more transparency with regard to the quantitative parameters used in the rating process."[65] Vernazza, Nielsen, and Vasileios demand "publishing a separate breakdown of the objective and subjective components of ratings, the minutes of the rating committees, and the voting records."[66]

---

63. International Organisation of Securities Commissions, *IOSCO Issues Final Code of Conduct Fundamentals for Credit Rating Agencies*, 2015, https://www.iosco.org/news/pdf/IOSCONEWS375.pdf, accessed July 30, 2015.

64. For example, see recital 42 and Section E, Annex 1, Transparency Report, par. 3 in Regulation (EC) No. 1060/2009 of the European Parliament and of the Council of 16 September 2009 on credit rating agencies.

65. J. Kiff, S. Nowak, and L. B. Schumacher, "Are Rating Agencies Powerful? An Investigation into the Impact and Accuracy of Sovereign Ratings," IMF Working Papers, 12/23 (Washington, DC: IMF, 2012).

66. D. Vernazza, E. Nielsen, and G. Vasileios, "The Damaging Bias of Sovereign Ratings," *UniCredit Global Themes Series*, no. 21 (March 26, 2014).

Rating agencies themselves have put great effort into publicizing the rating process.[67] Given the harsh criticism credit rating agencies faced during the crisis, some have described these efforts as a "pretty-looking PR campaign" to regain lost confidence and restore reputation, without having an effect on the agencies' actual practices.[68] The credit rating agencies' efforts emphasize their desire to appear as market institutions that reduce information asymmetries in financial markets. To fulfill this role it makes sense for the agencies to demonstrate their willingness to comply with the common value of transparency. If credit rating agencies failed to appear as transparent as possible, this would be in conflict with the dominant understanding of rating, undermining the credit rating agencies' legitimacy.

The goal of rating traceability via transparency about methods is a widely shared ideal. The objectivity of rating could be best achieved if rating becomes the result of verifiable statistical models and algorithms, as, for example, advocated by Nouriel Roubini.[69] But this agenda is premised on a probabilistic understanding of rating, which misunderstands rating. First, as noted in chapter 2, the rating process brings together questions of the willingness as well as the capacity to repay debt. Unlike calculation, qualitative and quantitative components are mixed. Second, ratings necessarily in-

---

67. For example, Moody's updated its sovereign rating methodology in September 2013: "The changes include more detail on how Moody's thinks about economic, institutional and fiscal strength, as well as vulnerability to shocks such as banking and foreign-exchange crises that could increase the risk of default." V. Batchelor and K. Nicholas, "Moody's Alters Sovereign Rating Method to Better Assess Risk," http://www.bloomberg.com/news/articles/2013-09-13/moodys-revises-sovereign-rating-method-to-better-assess-risk, accessed July 21, 2015.

68. Blodget, "Moody's Analyst Breaks Silence."

69. Roubini, "Rating Agencies Still Matter." Also see Nouriel Roubini and Stephen Mihm, *Crisis Economics: A Crash Course in the Future of Finance* (New York: Penguin, 2010).

volve judgment. They are not unambiguous and do not exist independently from interpretation. They are social constructions, products of deliberation. Third, predicting the future is a task involving great uncertainty.[70] Finally, if ratings were computable and predictable, there would be no market for credit rating agencies' ratings. As long as the ideal of making rating decisions traceable is nurtured by unachievable expectations that promote rating preciseness, correctness, and absence of errors, enhanced transparency of rating methods will be ineffective in fostering rating quality.

Advocates of results-based approaches have criticized the reforms for their focus on process. Enhancing the transparency of rating performance indicators, sometimes referred to as default history, is an output-oriented approach to rating agency regulation that has increased in popularity since the global financial crisis. The EU adopted such an approach with ESMA's establishment of a "Central Repository (CEREP) for publishing rating activity statistics and rating performance statistics of credit rating agencies."[71]

A valid measurement of rating performance presupposes that the credit rating agencies' predictions are not able to interact with the social reality ratings are trying to predict. The hit ratio of a meteorologist's predictions is a valid proxy for his or her ability, as

---

70. The agencies, as Abdelal and Blyth have suggested, engage in a process of "describing uncertainty as risk." This "may be a fiction," but it is a "necessary one." Abdelal and Blyth, "Just Who Put You in Charge?," 54. The agencies provide "estimates of certainty in an uncertain world," making financial innovation like structured finance possible. Abdelal and Blyth, 56. On this dynamic, and how it has transformed finance since the 1980s, see Alexandra Ouroussoff, *Wall Street at War: The Secret Struggle for the Global Economy* (Cambridge: Polity, 2010).

71. European Securities and Markets Authority, 2011. About the CEREP, see ESMA/2011/408.

a meteorologist cannot influence the weather he or she is trying to predict. The idea that a transparent evaluation of the credit rating agencies' track record is conducive to rating quality reveals a technical (and false) understanding of rating as a metric. It neglects that ratings, as social facts, are performative and can shape the social reality they are supposed to describe.[72] Instead of "measuring" credit risks like a "camera," ratings also shape them like an "engine" because they influence financial market actors' decisions.[73] For instance, if a sovereign rating downgrade leads to increased interest rates for a sovereign, its refinancing ability on bond markets deteriorates, increasing the probability of a sovereign default even more, creating a self-fulfilling prophecy.[74] Their pro-cyclical character turns ratings themselves into factors of systemic instability.[75] This has an implication for regulation. The impact of ratings on investors and issuers invalidates the notion of a supposedly independent measurement of rating performance. Applying new regulations that have a blind spot toward performativity reveals how the regulatory response can be undermined by it not being based in a social foundation understanding of rating. Regulators have not been able to cope successfully with market reflexivity, which confirms the "regulators' conundrum."[76]

72. Hiss and Rona-Tas, "The Role of Ratings in the Subprime Mortgage Crisis," 115–155.

73. D. MacKenzie, *An Engine, Not a Camera* (Cambridge, MA: MIT Press, 2006).

74. Gärtner and Griesbach, "Rating Agencies, Self-Fulfilling Prophecy and Multiple Equilibria?"

75. A. Sy, "The Systemic Regulation of Credit Rating Agencies and Rated Markets," IMF Working Papers, 09/129 (Washington, DC: IMF, 2009); B. Paudyn, "Credit Rating Agencies and the Sovereign Debt Crisis: Performing the Politics of Creditworthiness through Risk and Uncertainty," *Review of International Political Economy* 20, no. 4 (2013): 788–818.

76. B. Stellinga and D. Mügge, "The Regulator's Conundrum: How Market Reflexivity Limits Fundamental Financial Reform," *Review of International Po-*

What we see here is an understanding of credit rating agencies as neutral, informational intermediators between borrowers and lenders who are supposed to decrease information asymmetries in financial markets. The underlying assumption is market-centered, that objective knowledge about credit risk exists, which the agencies just have to find, process, and publish. The regulators' task is to make sure credit rating agencies are able to express this unbiased view by silencing the different noises generated by conflicts of interest or bad practices. The fact that rating is judgment remains, even if absolute transparency were realized.

Apart from the regulatory goals of increasing competition and transparency, in the wake of the global financial crisis attempts were made to reduce market and regulatory reliance on ratings in order to decrease the agencies' authority. For example, the Dodd-Frank Act prescribes the removal of references to ratings in financial market regulations.[77] Mandated by the G20, the Financial Stability Board (FSB) started an initiative to reduce reliance on credit rating agencies' ratings.[78] Similarly, in the scholarly literature "the withdrawal of rating-based regulations" and the abandonment of the credit rating agencies' quasi-regulatory position are seen as necessary conditions for a successful reform of the rating industry.[79]

In times of crisis, overreliance on rating can translate into fire sales of securities under downward rating pressure. Credit rating agencies' comments, announcements, outlook changes, and actual rating changes homogenize market participants' creditworthiness

---

litical Economy 24, no. 3 (2017): 3. Also see Stellinga, "Why Performativity Limits Credit Rating Reform," 20–41.

77. See Sec. 939–939A in Dodd-Frank, July 21, 2010.

78. Financial Stability Board, *Principles for Reducing Reliance on CRA Ratings*, 2010.

79. Darbellay, *Regulating Credit Rating Agencies*, 9.

perceptions and favor herd behavior—in the worst case, almost "off the cliff edge." Increasing pro-cyclicality, ratings become a factor of systemic risk.[80] Consequently, if reliance on credit rating agencies' ratings in micro-prudential regulations is reduced, rating actions will be less consequential, and herd behavior less likely, so the argument goes.

It has been difficult to abandon the hard wiring of ratings in regulations and reduce market reliance. Evidence suggests that reliance on credit rating agencies persists.[81] As noted earlier, when the Basel Committee for Banking Supervision (BCBS) presented its Basel IV proposals to take ratings out of regulations, market representatives opposed them strongly.[82] Eric Helleiner has characterized "the content of post-crisis international financial regulatory reforms," including those applying to the agencies, as "remarkably tame," noting that "the market-friendly nature of pre-crisis international financial standards" has only been "tweaked."[83]

An explanation for the FSB's lack of success concerns the practical difficulty of replacing ratings. There seem to be alternatives.[84] Incentivizing the use of alternatives to ratings, including the promotion of investors' due diligence, however, disregards the ratio-

---

80. Sy, "The Systemic Regulation of Credit Rating Agencies"; Paudyn, "Credit Rating Agencies and the Sovereign Debt Crisis."

81. Financial Stability Board, *Thematic Review on FSB Principles for Reducing Reliance on CRA Ratings*, Peer Review Report, 2014, 2.

82. S. Verma, *Bank Regulation: "Basel IV" Sparks Banker Fury* (London: Euromoney, 2015).

83. Eric Helleiner, *The Status Quo Crisis: Global Financial Governance after the 2008 Meltdown* (New York: Oxford University Press, 2014), 12. Also see 123.

84. Alternatives to CRAs' ratings are, for example, internal ratings of financial institutions, market-implied ratings, accountancy-based measures, OECD country risk classification (for sovereign ratings), or Central Credit Registers (for corporates). For further details, see European Commission (2015) Study on the Feasibility of Alternatives to Credit Ratings, Executive Summary, 4–6.

nale behind the use of ratings in disintermediated financial markets. Given the disappearance of the traditional role of banks in financial intermediation, the markets need judgmental intermediation between those having and those seeking funds. Effective credit rating agency regulation aimed at changing the status quo cannot circumvent these constitutive features of rating in disintermediated financial markets. Some judgments matter more than others. Homeostasis is still extant here.

Often neglected by advocates of the regulatory license hypothesis is that the market practice of using ratings preceded rating use by national regulators, supervisors, and central banks. Likewise, the Reform Act increased the number of NRSROs registered with the SEC with "licensing power" from three to about ten, but the market oligopoly has continued to exist largely unaffected.[85] The outsourcing of credit risk regulation to ratings has certainly reinforced the credit rating agencies' authority. However, if the root of the credit rating agencies' authority lies somewhere else than in its regulatory license, then a successful reduction of the regulatory reliance on ratings, even if practically feasible, will not end the agencies' authority.

IT WAS A close-run thing. But instead of irreversibly damaging their reputation—as most expected—the credit rating agencies succeeded in retaining their epistemic authority after an existential crisis. The agencies remain a key social fact of the capital markets. They demonstrated their continuing significance in the European sovereign debt crisis and again in the downgrading of the United States' top credit rating. What has also maintained the agencies,

---

85. SEC website, https://www.sec.gov/ocr/ocr-current-nrsros.html, accessed September 4, 2017.

despite the intent to the contrary, are the efforts to increase competition and transparency by regulation. Certainly, the scope and intensity of regulation have increased, to the cost of credit rating agencies, those who use their services, and the taxpayer who finances the regulatory authorities. What has not changed is the dominant understanding of rating underlying rating regulation. Treating ratings as unambiguous metrics, private goods, and independent and neutral third-party opinions has led, first, to failed efforts to regulate the rating agencies, and, second, to the regulators' unwillingness to interfere with rating analytics or to pursue other, more wholesale change, despite demonstrations of resolve in public.

Ratings are not material facts "out there," waiting to be discovered. Rating agencies create ratings; they are social constructions providing one possible, centralized interpretation of creditworthiness. Since the market accepts these ratings because it sees certain credit rating agencies as authoritative (and others as not), ratings become social facts—a commonly shared interpretation of the world. Rating is about judgment, providing authoritative opinions, and is a public good and a constitutive feature of disintermediated financial markets. These conclusions require us to reject the dominant market-centered understanding of rating and embrace the social foundations understanding advocated in this book.

7

Addendum

Convenient Villains and All-Purpose Bogeymen

French president Nicolas Sarkozy advised Hank
[Paulson, US Treasury secretary] to find a convenient villain to deflect the inevitable public backlash:
he suggested scapegoating the ratings agencies that
had slapped triple-A ratings on shoddy securities.
"You need a simple story, and I know you won't
want to blame the bankers," Sarkozy teased him.
— *Bernanke, Geithner, and Paulson,*
Firefighting: The Financial Crisis and Its Lessons, *2019*

The rating agencies have been the all-purpose
bogeymen for the crisis. They bear a heavy responsibility . . . but this exclusive focus obscures how the
problems are embedded in the whole system: the
big banks, accountancy firms, financial law firms,
investment firms, regulators, the financial press. . . .
The rating agencies have done us a disservice by
allowing so much of the blame to rest on them.
They are effectively protecting these other players—
who seem quite happy with this arrangement.
Meanwhile people at rating agencies go: "just blame
us, we're used to it."
— *William J. Harrington, formerly of Moody's,*
The Guardian, *December 17, 2012*

The broader puzzle motivating this book is my observation, in the case of the global financial crisis, that explanations for the crisis in finance have been focused away from finance itself, on to other institutions, whether government agencies or corporate service providers. The rating agencies were, of course, the prime target. My third or supplementary argument, which because it is so broad I present in this addendum, is about the continuing vitality of the exogenous view of crises. The argument is that comment by politicians, regulators, experts, the financial press, and the wider media identifying a bad guy, a villain, as we see with the rating agencies and the financial crisis, is best understood as part of a process of assuagement in a complex, massive failure like the global financial crisis. Focusing on the bad guy offers a way of relieving public and professional anger. In making this argument I am not suggesting, of course, that the agencies are blameless.

Broad processes such as financial innovation are, no doubt, challenging for most people to think about concretely, and perhaps suggest financial markets are themselves problematic. The search for bad guys and for developing limited "Band-Aid" solutions may, I suggest, be best interpreted to be about reducing the damage failure causes to collective belief in the coherence and legitimacy of the broader financial system. A narrative of assuagement that focuses on institutions held to be outside finance has the advantage of being concrete and specific, and focused on the failure of things other than the financial markets themselves. This external or exogenous view of the causes of crisis reinforces the idea that finance itself is not the problem, only the human institutions that interact with finance, such as government or the agencies.

The Bad Guy in the Black Hat

The politics of global finance seem different from those of other sectors.[1] In trade, the question of who gets what from international cooperation seems obvious. But coming to grips with the politics at stake in global finance is more challenging to many. Financial market participants tend to speak a language of their own, and unlike trade, finance lacks tangible referents like barrels of oil or pork bellies. Given this, and the unwillingness of most observers to see financial crises as social or political phenomena, it is no wonder that financial crises tend to produce a mythic culture at the center of which stands the bad guy in the black hat, to which all blame can conveniently be attached.[2]

Bad guys must be important to be taken seriously. Hank Paulson, U.S. Treasury secretary, made it clear when presenting the policy statement of the President's Working Group on Financial Markets in March 2008 that in the midst of the current market turbulence, officials, politicians, and their advisers believed credit rating agencies "play a major role in financial markets," and that the work of the agencies must be improved in terms of the specific challenges faced in rating complex financial instruments like structured securities.[3]

---

1. This chapter draws on Timothy J. Sinclair, "The Queen and the Perfect Bicycle," *Inside Story*, August 12, 2009, http://inside.org.au/the-queen-and-the-perfect-bicycle/; and Timothy J. Sinclair, "Round Up the Usual Suspects: Blame and the Subprime Crisis," *New Political Economy* 15, no. 1 (March 2010): 91–107.

2. Simon Jenkins, "A Tribunal Must Tell Us What to Fix. And Whom to Punish," *The Guardian*, September 17, 2008, www.guardian.co.uk/commentisfree/2008/sep/17/economics.banking.

3. Henry H. Paulson, press release, March 13, 2008, www.treas.gov/press/releases/hp872.htm, accessed October 13, 2008.

The increasingly volatile nature of markets in the post–Bretton Woods world of international capital mobility created a crisis in relations between the agencies and governments, which sought to monitor their performance and stimulate reform in their procedures. This helped drive the "moral panic" about agency performance in subprime mortgage finance—a quiet panic among professionals that became increasingly noisy as it moved into media accounts of the crisis.[4] But in pursuing improvement in the rating system, policymakers need to appreciate the limits to rating. Expectations of the agencies are founded on a market-centered rationalist or machinelike understanding of the workings of capital markets, and on an exogenous understanding of the causes of financial crisis. This worldview implies that a single correct rating can be determined, and that finding this correct answer is a technical matter. But a more accurately social (and dynamic) view of markets and financial crises makes the challenge of effective rating more daunting.

The record of financial crises shows they are always shocking. Typically, crises occur after long periods of affluent self-confidence. Pride comes before the fall. The reversal they represent seems incomprehensible to those involved, never mind the general public. Typical of each episode are efforts to identify villains, often several, who could be held responsible for the crisis. This pattern is evident in the event that set the standard against which all financial crises are measured: the Great Depression of the 1930s. At the height of the Depression a quarter of American workers were

---

4. S. Cohen, *Folk Devils and Moral Panics*, 3rd ed. (London: Routledge, 2002), xxiii; and Colin Hay, "Mobilization through Interpellation: James Bulger, Juvenile Crime and the Construction of a Moral Panic," *Social and Legal Studies* 4 (1995): 197–223.

unemployed.[5] The New York Stock Exchange did not return to its summer 1929 level until the early 1950s, almost a quarter century after the crash of October 1929.[6] Greedy, unscrupulous bankers were the main bad guys of the Great Depression.

Financial crises did not, however, start in the twentieth century. The Dutch "tulip mania" of the 1630s, in which tulip bulbs dramatically appreciated in value, is usually cited as the first boom and bust. At the time, tulips were exotic imports from the eastern Mediterranean. "Mass mania" for the bulbs led to massive price inflation, making bulbs worth the equivalent of $50,000 or more each. When the crash came and the bubble deflated "not with a whimper but with a bang," many who had invested their life savings in tulips lost everything.[7] Mass default ensured a depression in the Netherlands in the years after 1637.[8] More recently, the 1907 financial panic came about after the failure of a trust company at the center of fervent Wall Street speculation.[9] Calamity was avoided by cooperation between major banks, led by J. P. Morgan, at the time the world's best-known and most powerful financier.

After the Great Depression and World War II, the Bretton Woods regime was created to bring greater order to the global financial system. As much a political as a financial framework, Bretton Woods was intended to avoid rapid and unsettling economic adjustments within countries. The hope was this would avoid the sort of economic problems that contributed to World War II, and that would,

---

5. J. K. Galbraith, *The Great Crash of 1929* (New York: Mariner, 1997 [1958]), 168.

6. Dow Jones, 2009 www.djindexes.com, accessed March 3, 2009.

7. J. K. Galbraith, *A Short History of Financial Euphoria* (London: Penguin, 1993), 4.

8. Galbraith, 26–33.

9. R. F. Bruner and S. D. Carr, *The Panic of 1907: Lessons Learned from the Market's Perfect Storm* (New York: Wiley, 2007).

some feared, increase support for the communist system in Russia. Although the intent behind Bretton Woods was to avoid crises and the political conflict that followed, despite US assistance, Bretton Woods institutions had relatively few resources. Given the considerable protectionism in trade, countries were frequently either in sizeable surplus or deficit in their national accounts. This led to panic-driven efforts to restore balance to their payments, aggravating relations with other states.

The Bretton Woods system, fixed exchange rates, and controls over the movement of capital were gradually abandoned in the developed world in the fifteen years after 1970, although the EU sought to establish exchange rate stability within the union. What emerged was a system in which floating exchange rates were increasingly the norm in developed countries, and in which capital could flow freely around the world to find the sources of highest return. Although a floating exchange rate regime should rapidly adjust to reflect the changing economic conditions in a country (real interest rates, inflation, profit margins, regulations, political stability), this proved less than perfect. The 1980s was marked by a series of currency crises, as the values of major currencies like the Japanese yen appreciated, causing trouble for their trade partners. Perhaps the most dramatic of these events was the Exchange Rate Mechanism (ERM) crisis of 1992, in which currency traders, including George Soros, placed bets on the ability of the British government to keep the pound sterling within the European ERM. During the crisis, the British government had to abandon defending sterling, which depreciated substantially and was expelled from the ERM. Some people blamed Soros for the crisis.

The Asian financial crisis of 1997–1998 was the culmination of a boom in Asia that led to what in hindsight turned out to be excessive short-term lending and risky pegging of national currencies to the US dollar, a problem also for Argentina in 2001. Like Holland in the 1630s, the result of the crisis was economic depression in some countries, notably Indonesia, where the price of basic foodstuffs and other costs increased dramatically. The Asian crisis, like the global financial crisis, led to criticism of lax regulation, fraud, corruption, and "crony capitalism." In Malaysia, despite a barrage of Western criticism, controls on the movement of capital were reintroduced until the market panic eased. Given the regional nature of this crisis, the politics of blame were intense, leading to a legacy of polarization and bitterness. With the Asia crisis, it became clear that the ideal of a smoothly functioning financial system is far from an accomplished fact. However, with time, as was the case with prior crises, the motivation to reform and control volatility subsided.

In and Out

How we understand causes of financial crises has a major effect on who gets blamed for them. It is possible to identify two main ways of understanding crises that compete for scholarly and political preeminence. The first of these has dominated economic thought about finance for more than thirty years and has had a major influence on policymakers. This stream of thought I call the exogenous approach to financial crisis. In this tradition, financial crisis is a deviation from the normal state of the market. Given that they assumed markets worked efficiently, this tradition focused on "external" causes, especially government policy, as the instigator of crisis. Indeed, on the assumptions of this approach a culprit other than the markets must exist. One recent account has drawn a distinction between human and market failure, noting that analysts concur on the basic problem, agreeing that the former was the cause and not the latter.[10] So the markets were not the problem for exogenous thinkers. Rating agencies, although endogenous to finance, are cast as outside the markets, and therefore can easily be blamed.

As we have seen, exogenous accounts of financial crisis assume that market participants are constantly adjusting their behavior—whether they buy or sell financial instruments like bonds and stocks—following the Efficient Markets Hypothesis, based on new information from outside the market. The idea of a "bubble economy," in which assets like houses, stocks, and oil futures deviate from some true value to a higher, false value, is impossible. There can be no "true value" other than what the market is prepared to pay.

The endogenous account, by contrast, says that financial crises begin with finance itself. Keynes provided what remains perhaps the best intuitive illustration of the importance of this internal, social understanding of finance and financial crises in his tabloid beauty contest metaphor discussed earlier.[11] George Cooper has argued that traditional assumptions made about markets and their tendency to equilibrium between demand and supply do not work for assets like houses, art, and financial instruments like stocks, bonds, and derivatives.[12] In the market for goods, greater demand can be met with greater supply or higher prices. But this simple economic logic does not work for assets. Instead, demand often grows in response to price increases for assets. The "animal spirits" identified by Keynes, and discussed by George Akerlof and Robert

---

10. Laurence J. Kotlikoff, "The Big Con—Reassessing the 'Great Recession' and Its 'Fix,'" NBER Working Paper 25213 (Cambridge, MA: National Bureau of Economic Research, November 2018).

11. George Akerlof and Robert Shiller, *Animal Spirits: How Human Psychology Drives the Economy and Why It Matters for Global Capitalism* (Princeton, NJ: Princeton University Press, 2009), 133.

12. George Cooper, *The Origin of Financial Crises: Central Banks, Credit Bubbles and the Efficient Market Fallacy* (Hampshire, UK: Harriman House, 2008), 9–13.

Shiller, do not produce stability in the market for assets in the same way they do in the market for goods. In the absence of equilibrium, there is no limit to the expansion of market enthusiasm for financial assets or houses, producing what we have come to call a "bubble" economy.

The dominant calculative techniques used in structured finance were key to triggering the financial crisis. Rather than discrediting structured finance as a form of financial innovation, these techniques have allowed supporters to claim that the techniques were wrong, not structured finance itself. Watson has focused on Li's Gaussian Copula, which he suggests has "no genuinely economic content" and is therefore, in the terms discussed here, symptomatic of the shift to an exogenous approach, or what he calls a "distinctly uneconomic economics."[13] Get the calculative techniques right, get the numbers right, get the rating agencies right, and everything can go back to normal is the implication Watson highlights.

Perception of Rating Failure

The global financial crisis, like Enron before it, has been traumatic for the major rating agencies. Moody's, S&P, and Fitch worked hard at creating their reputation for impartiality over the past century. In some situations where people surrender their own powers of judgment to an institution or to a group, the surrender may be quite fragile, as in the case of a fad or fashion.[14] Or it may be a largely public posture. The circumstances, including the longevity of the rating agencies, have made their authoritative niche more resilient than

---

13. Watson, *Uneconomic Economics*, 25.
14. S. Bikchandani, D. Hirshleifer, and I. Welch, "A Theory of Fads, Fashion, Custom, and Cultural Change as Informational Cascades," *Journal of Political Economy* 100, no. 5 (1992): 1016.

most other nonstate institutions. Their position within the capital markets provides them with considerable resources. The reputation of the Big Three has been constructed over time through a combination of serving a need between buyers and sellers and providing that information in a reliable way, generating epistemic authority. Even if individuals are skeptical about the rating agencies, they cannot assume others have the same view. Because of this risk, skeptical individuals have incentives to act based on the assumption that others will use the rating agencies as benchmarks—as what Searle calls social facts.

Given that the reputational assets of the rating agencies are not natural, but reflect a process of construction, the question of the deconstruction or degrading of those assets is important. Rating agencies will, like any other institution, lose authority and power systematically if major events like financial crises occur that they are widely thought to have misunderstood, generating a crisis of confidence in them, as happened to Arthur Andersen in relation to Enron Corporation. Near-continuous expressions of concern about rating performance—about how good or bad the rating agencies are at their business—are normal. Newspapers, magazines, and online sites debate the performance of the agencies daily. This talk became very "noisy" in Stanley Cohen's sense, during the failure of Enron Corporation and again during the global financial crisis.

Unlike wars and famine, the global financial crisis and how it was caused seem to have caught the governing elites in rich countries completely unawares. The crisis and the deep recession it generated led to dismay and at times panic as the depth of the problem revealed itself, especially in September 2008 with the bankruptcy of investment bank Lehman Brothers. The claim made about the pathology of securitization is that it led to a breakdown in the relationship between the originators of mortgages and those in the financial markets creating and trading in the bonds and derivatives that pooled the stream of income from these mortgages. Because people in the financial markets were so distant from the actual credit risk of the individual mortgage payers and were supposedly poorly advised by credit rating agencies, they underestimated the riskiness of the assets. This meant the financial system was full of "toxic assets," and once this was fully appreciated by markets in the summer of 2007 as a result of increasing mortgage defaults by subprime borrowers, panic developed, followed by the collapse of major financial institutions, worldwide government intervention to prop up the markets, and the subsequent recession.

But the standard account reproduces the assumptions of the exogenous approach to financial crises. It suggests that the crisis occurred because some people were not doing their jobs properly, were intervening in finance ineptly, and that if we can just make sure people do what they are supposed to do, and do that well, another financial crisis like this can be avoided.

As I noted earlier in this book, the "bad news" about subprime lending was actually modest in summer 2007, predicting a higher rate of mortgage foreclosures than anticipated, but not a crisis. But in combination with the repo funding system, this proved enough to cause panic in the markets and bring them to a halt over the next year or so. The panic, which so typically follows financial expansions, created widespread uncertainty about the quality of financial institutions and their balance sheets. It is this uncertainty, especially in the repo markets, that effectively brought the financial markets to a halt, forcing government intervention. Exogenous assumptions about financial crises could not assimilate the valuation crisis as a crisis within markets. Given the hegemony of exogenous views of the causes for financial crises, manias, panics, and crashes *have to* be explained as a result of specific failures rather than understood as the result of social interactions at the height of a boom. It is necessary, given this worldview, to find those institutions that did not do their jobs properly, shame them, and make sure they do right in future. The crisis had to have external causes. Rating agency involvement in the subprime mortgage securities market became an attractive culprit for blame.

What unites Enron with the global financial crisis is the important role of extreme forms of financial innovation. In the second case, among securities created out of underlying loans to residential mortgage borrowers, a small proportion had relatively weak personal credit ratings. The holders of these structured securities had little understanding of the quality of the underlying assets. What distinguishes the global financial crisis from Enron, and made the global financial crisis systemic, is not the innovation itself but the corrosive effect of market uncertainty on valuations in the securities market. It was easy to dismiss Enron as a gang of bad guys engaging in illegal market manipulation in far-off Texas, a "flyover" state. But the essence of the global financial crisis is not illegality or the bankruptcy of the poor, but uncertainty about financial engineering at the heart of the global financial system, and the collective shared fear this created. It was as if the suspension of disbelief that occurs in the cinema when a movie is good has been shattered by poor dialogue, bad special effects, and weak acting.

It comes as no surprise, then, that the rating agencies were subject to unprecedented criticism and investigation in the midst of the crisis, as we have seen. This is despite, as some raters see it, their responsiveness in the changing circumstances.[15] Congressional committees, the SEC, the European Parliament and Commission—

---

15. Interview with Ian Linnell, global analytical head, Fitch Ratings, Canary Wharf, London, October 2, 2014.

all conducted investigations. The moral panic about rating is an interesting development, given that the rating agency business has been open to much greater competition since the Credit Rating Agency Reform Act of 2006. It suggests that the movement from regulation observed during the Bretton Woods era to self-regulation adopted since the end of it—from "police patrol" to "fire alarm" approaches—has not eliminated the key role of the state in financial markets. Governments are still expected by their citizens to deal with failure, and when necessary act as lenders of last resort and investigate culprits, and they know it. What seems apparent in the moral panic is an initiative to discipline the agencies pursued by a state, using public shaming as a governance instrument, intent on improving performance.[16] The identification of the agencies as villains in the context of elite and public dismay over global markets echoes the vilification endured by US investment banks in the 1930s.[17]

Since the 1930s, financial crises have almost always been accompanied by public controversy over who was at fault. Before the 1930s, governments were not generally held responsible for economic conditions, but since then the public have expected governments to manage problems in the economic and financial system. Inevitably, efforts to defuse or redirect blame have developed. During the Asia crisis, corruption or "crony capitalism" in Asian governments and among their business leaders was held responsible, even though just a few years before "Asian values" were supposedly responsible for the unprecedented growth in the region. During the Enron scandal of 2001/2002, auditors were blamed for not

---

16. Michael Moran, *The British Regulatory State: High Modernism and Hyper-Innovation* (Oxford: Oxford University Press, 2003), 1–11.

17. Galbraith, *The Great Crash of 1929*.

revealing the financial chicanery of the corporation. The global financial crisis has been no different. Many have been blamed, but no one more so than the agencies.

Portraying the Agencies

Evidence of a determination to assign blame to the agencies for the global financial crisis is widespread in the years after 2007. Even as late as 2016 articles about the "indisputable role" of the agencies in creating the crisis were being published in the press and in online news sources.[18] These and other sources lamented the "unfinished business" of rating agency regulatory reform.[19] Charles Tilly suggests that "blame activates sharper distinctions between a worthy us and an unworthy them than credit does."[20] Perhaps this is so because of a sense of a broken promise from the agencies, that they would turn uncertainty into specified risk, but failed to do so. It turned out in fact that they did the opposite. Tilly explains the vehemence of the blame process by arguing that establishing blame separates two moral settings from one another. Blaming the other justifies "my own distinction from the culprit's world."[21] This makes sense of the

---

18. Deena Zaidi, "The Indisputable Role of the Credit Ratings Agencies in the 2008 Collapse, and Why Nothing Has Changed," *Truthout*, March 19, 2016, https://truthout.org/articles/the-indisputable-role-of-credit-ratings-agencies-in-the-2008-collapse-and-why-nothing-has-changed/, accessed October 16, 2019.

19. Gretchen Morgenson, "Ratings Agencies Still Coming Up Short, Years after Crisis," *New York Times*, January 8, 2016, https://www.nytimes.com/2016/01/10/business/ratings-agencies-still-coming-up-short-years-after-crisis.html, accessed October 16, 2019. Also see Gretchen Morgenson and Joshua Rosner, *Reckless Endangerment: How Outsized Ambition, Greed, and Corruption Led to Economic Armageddon* (New York: Times Books, 2011).

20. Charles Tilly, *Credit and Blame* (Princeton, NJ: Princeton University Press, 2008), ix.

21. Tilly, 6.

willingness of other members of the financial community and of elected officials to blame the agencies, lest perhaps someone turn the blame on them or the system itself.

Stories of blame people tell each other about events like the global financial crisis are important ways in which we interpret and remember these events. But, of course, such stories "rework and simplify" the social processes involved, just as a movie reworks and simplifies the book it is based on.[22] Stories are not neutral. They "include strong imputations of responsibility, and thus lend themselves to moral evaluations."[23] As in the story of the rating agencies and the financial crisis, "stories inevitably minimize or ignore the intricate webs of cause and effect that actually produce human social life," such as the global financial crisis.[24]

The agencies were first portrayed in a feature documentary on the causes of the financial crisis, *Inside Job*, released in 2010.[25] As I mentioned above, the agencies also featured in the drama *The Big Short* in 2015, in which a bumbling senior rating official explains why her firm has rated some structured finance instruments, seemingly under pressure to maintain market share. Perhaps the most intense focus specifically on the agencies in this format was the hourlong documentary *The Power of the Rating Agencies*, made by Dutch broadcaster VPRO in 2012, in their *Backlight* series.[26]

---

22. Tilly, 21.
23. Tilly, 21.
24. Tilly, 21.
25. Directed by Charles Ferguson and distributed by Sony Pictures Classics.
26. VPRO are nontabloid in approach and very well resourced. The crew visited several countries in the making of this production. I am interviewed in this documentary, as is David Levey, former managing director at Moody's of European sovereign ratings. I have used the documentary makers' subtitles for translations into English. Available at https://www.youtube.com/watch?v=eyiy9TQNQYQ&list

Ironically, given the epigraph at the start of this chapter, the documentary begins with President Sarkozy of France, seemingly distraught at news of the 2011 downgrading of France's sovereign rating by S&P.[27] The narrative develops the idea that we should all be astonished at the "sudden, apparently limitless" power of the rating agencies, which was somehow previously hidden, given their errors in the global financial crisis. Where the documentary relies on expertise, including people cited in this book, it is mostly thoughtful and incisive.[28] The documentary also features interviews with a small-town mayor in Portugal, a blogger and trader in New York, and a retired lawyer living near Lake Tahoe, who had invested in Lehman bonds. The interview with two Portuguese journalists features comment on the rise in populist thinking and anger that developed in Portugal after a sovereign downgrade. One of these journalists asks if the rating agencies care about the country and people, asking if the agencies are concerned about the ten million inhabitants of the country, or are just trying to prove something to someone by downgrading. The Portuguese mayor stresses the lack of knowledge the agencies had of his town and the injustice of the sovereign ceiling that limited his town's rating, suggesting the agencies were the "main cause" of the global financial crisis in any case. The mayor then goes on to tell the camera we are in a new war, one about finance, in which Europe should develop new ways to take care of European concerns. A German commentator makes some thoughtful comments about

---

=PLuECoz9_QThSQUiuXN3gxK7sWvvqkDJmJ&index=7&t=2463s, accessed October 22, 2019.

27. Like the US sovereign downgrading, the lowering of France's rating was also accompanied by a controversy about an "error" in S&P's analysis.

28. In addition to Levey, Jerome Fons, who appears at some length in the documentary, was interviewed by the author for this book.

his concerns about lack of consistent criteria and conflicts of interest in the agencies, but then speculates on whether recent downgrades of European states are objective or "based on political pressure or strategies to keep Europe as small as possible." The retired lawyer, Ron Grassi, talked about his investment in Lehman bonds, and how he saw the rating of the bonds as "like a report card," and his astonishment when he lost his investment.[29] Grassi discussed his frustrations at the lack of prosecutions of those responsible for the financial crisis, and how "sometimes you have to put your foot down . . . the ball somehow dropped in our lap and we're stuck with it. Let's carry it." Grassi sued Moody's.[30] Fons, formerly of Moody's, suggested that what could change for the agencies is one of these suits being successful, because it would impact on the reputation and finances of the agencies, and "they could disappear . . . that's what could change the industry."[31]

Although Grassi could not make his case, and nobody else achieved the outcome Fons suggested was possible, the VPRO documentary

---

29. Drawing an analogy between grades in school and ratings is perhaps based on both these things using similar notation. But school grades are about past behavior. Ratings are about predicting the future. Ratings are more analogous to letters of recommendation than grades.

30. Grassi's legal action failed on appeal in late 2013. See "Ronald Grassi v. Moody's Investors Service, 11–17455 (9th Cir. 2013)," Court Listener, https://www.courtlistener.com/opinion/1042795/ronald-grassi-v-moodys-investors-services/, accessed October 21, 2019.

31. They could have perhaps, but they did not. Even the substantial settlements with the US Department of Justice did not trigger the outcome Fons anticipated. Legal action in relation to Puerto Rico municipal bond defaults is ongoing as of this writing. Richard Lawless, "'Small Claims Court' Lawsuits Could Cost Wall Street's Credit Rating Agencies Billions," *Rockland County Times*, December 5, 2019, https://www.rocklandtimes.com/2019/12/05/small-claims-court-lawsuits-could-cost-wall-streets-credit-rating-agencies-billions/, accessed December 7, 2019. Rockland County is in the Hudson River valley, north of New York City. The legal case was heard in California Superior Court.

should be understood as one moment among many in which blame was publicly attributed to the agencies, allowing the rest of us and the financial system itself to point the finger toward specific actions of a chosen culprit, rather than identifying the complex chains of cause and effect that actually produced the crisis.

INTERPRETATIONS OF THE global financial crisis are shaped by two very different understandings of financial crisis. The first, the exogenous approach, sees finance itself as a natural phenomenon, a smoothly oiled machine that every now and then gets messed up by the government, or events that nobody can anticipate, like war or famine. The other perspective, the endogenous, argues that the machinelike view of finance is mythic. Like all other human institutions, finance is made by people, in which collective understandings, norms, and assumptions give rise periodically to manias, panics, and crashes. On this account, financial crises are normal. What is not normal, concede those who support the endogenous perspective, is the expansion of financial crises into global events that threaten to destabilize world politics, as did the Great Depression of the 1930s or the global financial crisis that began in 2007.

The impulse to moral panic, to suggest that an institution has let us down, seems to follow most obviously from the exogenous approach. The endogenous thinkers know finance has a tendency to fall into crisis all on its own. The exogenous account, because it is premised on a market-centered, nonsocial, utopian image of finance as a smoothly functioning machine, must try to pin the blame for problems on deviance, on the failure of some to do their jobs properly, rather than on the periodically self-destructive properties of the system of global finance as a feature of the social world.

Governments, whether they like it or not, know they have responsibility for financial stability, and they have become adept at identifying and disciplining institutions that do not seem to serve their purpose within the financial system. As a result, "witch hunts" will continue to be a key feature of the fallout from financial crises, as governments attempt to offload as much of the liability for crises as possible.

The less important conclusion to be derived is that reforms are required to make global finance "work better." The more substantial conclusion is that global finance does not work as we think it works, that the most important dynamics are intersubjective or collectively shared ideas, and that, just like a Hollywood movie's box office takings, success cannot be guaranteed by mobilizing resources or technical skill. Given the reluctance of government regulators, market participants, and academics to confront the inherently social, relational character of global finance, we will continue to see efforts to vilify convenient institutions like the rating agencies when future crises emerge. These comments should not be read as an effort to exonerate the agencies from their role in the crisis, but only from the exaggerated claims made about them in the historical record, much of which expects much more precision and prescience than the social foundations of rating allow.

8

I'll Be Gone. You'll Be Gone.

When a particularly troubling fact came up in due diligence . . . a whispered "IBG YBG" among the banking team members would ensure that a way would be found to do the business, even if investors, or [the bank,] would pay the price down the road. Don't sweat it, was the implication, we'll all be gone by then.

—*Jonathan A. Knee,* The Accidental Investment Banker

Fall down seven times, get up eight.

—*Edo era aphorism, cited by Richard J. Samuels,* 3.11: Disaster and Change in Japan, *2013*

Now that more knowledge has been gleaned of the sorts of prices that lack credence, we are told, it is much easier to plug a more reasonable set of numbers into the valuation model. . . . This has allowed the argument to be made that with better information to hand about the structure of securities that delivers robust valuations, the securitization process should start again.

—*Matthew Watson,* Uneconomic Economics and the Crisis of the Model World, *2014*

More than a decade on from the global financial crisis and it is possible to say the major American rating agencies have never had it so good. They experienced tough times during the global financial crisis, but the Big Three have never been bigger or richer. They earn returns like the very best companies in the world. But, as this book has suggested, the world of global finance is a volatile one, and the agencies never know what set of circumstances is going to set off the next round of attacks on their franchise, nor which scandal might reveal a smoking gun, creating the basis for their termination, like that of Arthur Andersen.[1] Rating may look like a calm and even bookish industry, but that has been untrue for many years. Have the agencies learned from this experience? Will a new, more reflective rating industry emerge in the coming years, to serve as an antidote to extreme forms of financial innovation not yet invented? Will the agencies return to the conservative approach to rating established by John Moody more than a century ago?

Puzzles and Arguments

I explored three puzzles in this book. The first puzzle is why the agencies put their franchise at such risk prior to the crisis. Bad choices by institutions are quite normal, the substance of everyday life, and are therefore not puzzling in themselves. What is

---

1. The global pandemic that emerged in 2020 is the latest example of a set of events that threaten the agencies. See Huw Jones, "EU Watchdog Cautions Rating Agencies over Knee-Jerk Downgrades in Pandemic," Reuters, April 9, 2020, https://www.reuters.com/article/health-coronavirus-eu-regulator/eu-watchdog -cautions-rating-agencies-over-knee-jerk-downgrades-in-pandemic -idUSL5N2BX383, accessed September 25, 2020.

puzzling is when institutions make choices that seem, at least to the outside observer, to undermine their very reason for being. The rating agencies did this when they decided to advise their clients on the design of structured financial products that would achieve certain rating outcomes. This active role robbed the agencies of their established image as putatively disinterested parties, exposing them to accusations of partiality. This mostly took the public form of criticism of the conflict of interest inherent in the agencies taking payment from issuers for rating their bond issues. Why did the agencies take such massive risks with their franchise? Why did they not see this activity as potentially self-destructive? What was it that pushed these institutions, which had been steadfastly conservative for decades, to change their behavior so dramatically?

The second puzzle is how it is that the agencies managed to survive. Despite undermining their franchise by advising issuers on how to structure their issues to achieve specific ratings, they managed to avoid the fate that befell Arthur Andersen when it surrendered its CPA license in 2002 following the collapse of Enron Corporation. Indeed, the agencies have thrived since the crisis and demonstrated their renewed relevance during the European sovereign debt crisis that began in 2010. Why have the agencies survived seemingly unscathed, and have not been displaced or replaced by alternatives? Why have reform measures been so insubstantial? What are the prospects for the development of rating agencies in ways that make them return to a disinterested, countercyclical role that offers assurance to investors and public goods to society in terms of dampening market volatility?

The final puzzle is why the exogenous approach to understanding financial crises has continued to dominate the interpretation of the global financial crisis and the role of the agencies in the crisis. Given the scale and gravity of the crisis you might think an approach that offered a more systemic account of the crisis, that considered what was wrong with finance itself, would have become the mainstream or hegemonic interpretation, as occurred in the wake of the Great Depression. But this did not occur following the crisis that began in 2007. Instead of criticism of the degree to which society had become enthralled to finance, a way of making money with a known history of boom and bust, someone was found to blame. The exogenous approach to crisis remains the dominant view, and it continues to shape the collective understanding of the role of the agencies in the crisis.

Why did the agencies risk their franchise by switching to an advisory role, telling clients what they needed, and helping issuers obtain the ratings they required to create their structured finance products? What we need to get to grips with is what dislocated a long entrenched conservative rating mentality, a system and set of habits that had been established in these Wall Street institutions for decades. Why did the agencies embrace their changed role in securitized finance, even at the risk of destroying their rating franchise? My argument is that after the Enron disaster the agencies were uncertain about the rating business. They did not know what disasters lay around the next corner for them, given financial innovation. Their old model of how to operate no longer seemed relevant in these circumstances. Moody's canvassed market opinion about themselves and their output around this time. They might have stuck to their guns, or even become more conservative. But they did not. They changed a great deal in ways that made them almost unrecognizable.

Compounding this acute uncertainty was the rise of Fitch. Fitch changed a comfortable duopoly into a three-way oligopoly, making the agencies acutely sensitive to the shrinkage of their market share. Under the duopoly, Moody's and S&P were guaranteed to rate an issue, given the norm of two ratings per security. But that same norm meant one of the now three major agencies would miss out on the business once Fitch became a viable choice for issuers. If Fitch had not managed to become a member of what became the Big Three, the agencies may well have taken a more arm's-length relationship to structured finance, and it may never have become the business it became.

My second argument concerns the survival of the agencies. While the agencies failed, they did not die, as did Enron and Enron's audit firm Arthur Andersen. Moody's, S&P, and Fitch remain highly profitable. There may be elements of atonement or redemption about the survival of the agencies, but it is the continued functioning of the agencies that is most interesting, despite the odds stacked against them. How did these institutions that have been accused of terrible wrongdoing, incompetence, and corruption go on, and what marks out this persistence from the institutions that did not survive?

There is a two-pronged explanation to the persistence of the agencies. The first aspect concerns homeostasis. We do not have institutions that do what they do better than the rating agencies, despite whatever failings we attribute to them. The other dimension to survival of the agencies is the continuing dominance of the Big Three. The top agencies, Moody's, S&P, and Fitch, have not given way to the many smaller, less prominent agencies in the years since the crisis began, despite blame being directed toward the Big Three and efforts to open the rating market by authorities in the United States and Europe. The continued dominance of the Big Three reflects the necessity in ratings of some judgements having more weight than others. This is what market participants actually want. This bias to a small set of rating agencies is essential if ratings are to have any weight or authority to investors. Concentration of market share in a few hands reflects what ratings provide to those who use them. Reputation is exclusive and favors incumbents.

My final argument, presented in the addendum in chapter 7, about the continuing vitality of the exogenous view of crises, is that comment by politicians, regulators, experts, the financial press, and the wider media identifying a bad guy, a villain, as we see with the rating agencies and financial crisis, is best understood as part of a process of assuagement in a complex, massive failure like the global financial crisis. Focusing on the bad guy offers a way of relieving public and professional anger. In making this argument I am not suggesting that the agencies are blameless. The search for bad guys and for developing limited "Band-Aid" solutions is about reducing the damage failure causes to the collective belief in the coherence and legitimacy of the broader system. A strategy of assuagement that focuses on institutions outside finance has the advantage of being concrete and specific, and focused on the failure of things other than the core financial markets themselves. This external or exogenous view of the causes of crisis reinforces the idea that finance itself is not the problem, only the human institutions that interact with finance.

Were the Rating Agencies to Blame?

At least three things were key to the direct contribution of the rating agencies to the germination of the crisis. First, there is the problem of how to incorporate future events into ratings. Ratings cannot just assume imminent Armageddon. Issuing ratings anticipates some sort of normal, reasonable future. If ratings always assumed Armageddon, other things being equal, very few ratings, if any, would be anything other than speculative grade. Like everyone else prior to the onset of crisis, the agencies assumed a large measure of continuity. They factored in business cycle downturns, as they have done with rating corporate bonds for decades. What they did not do is anticipate a deep, geographically widespread market crisis. Assuming things will be largely similar in the future, and so underestimating change, proved to be a mistake. This is the sort of error many businesses and governments make. It is hard to predict the future and even harder to predict the specific characteristics of the future.

The second contribution made by the agencies to the development of the crisis is the curious fact that the rating agencies were not rating the quality of the original financial assets, the mortgages that underpinned RMBS. Although most people assume this is what they were doing, the agencies were rating something else. The agencies were rating claims on the flows of funds that emerged from these mortgages. The logic of this is that claims could be legally distinguished one from another using trusts, which are characterized by claims to assets organized in tranches. Some tranches of bonds had stronger legal claims than others to the flow of funds (and so would receive cash first from people paying their mortgages). This was the basis for awarding the strongest claims the AAA rating. The idea was that they would never fail to pay, even if lower-rated tranches defaulted. This model of credit protection turned out to be unreliable as conditions worsened, and so proved a mistake.

The third contribution, what I give most weight to, is the role of the agencies in their own undermining. The conventional explanation suggests that the agencies were simply going after the money, and so rating everything strongly to earn high fees. A variant of the greed argument uses the language of conflict of interest. It focuses on the fact that the agencies are paid by the issuers of debt. The argument is that this incentivizes the agencies to inflate ratings to keep those who pay for ratings happy. This is a popular argument, although it does not explain why conflict of interest is suddenly a problem in 2007 despite existing since the late 1960s. We need to understand more than greed. This is not what happened. Rather, I suggest, *the agencies stopped working as judges of the process and started working as advisers to the process.* The key role of the agencies during the twentieth century had been to offer disinterested advice, to play the role of referee or judge in the debt markets. This role is like that of auditors. Now, the agencies started to provide advice to issuers on how to organize financial contracts to meet the thresholds for the different tranches and their respective flows of funds. By advising on the construction of financial instruments like this the agencies threatened their standing as disinterested judges of the financial instruments of others. The lack of critical distance fed back into the failure to anticipate the crisis, weak scrutiny of the originating credit quality, and, very importantly, skepticism about their judgments at key moments in the crisis, especially once the rhetoric of conflict of interest had been stoked up by critics of the agencies. Not sticking closely to their core role proved to be a catastrophic mistake by the agencies.

Is There a Role for Government in the Future of Rating?

Historically, governments have had little role in the rating industry. Apart from the 1975 introduction of NRSRO standing in the United States, the agencies were not meaningfully regulated until the Credit Rating Agency Reform Act of 2006. Most of that, along with the applicable provisions of Dodd-Frank, which followed five years later, was not substantive, but best characterized as regulative box ticking. Where regulative rule box ticking became constitutive, as it did with Dodd-Frank's effort to overcome the agencies' free speech rights, these provisions were not systematically advanced and did not survive long.

Of all government agencies around the world, the SEC has shown the most understanding of the dilemmas in the rating world. It is less clear that the challenges of rating are understood well by other agencies. Few politicians seem to have a clear and effective grasp on what rating is and how it works, even if they do have a good understanding of financial innovation.[2] On one hand, in this context, building a new international organization to regulate the agencies seems like a bad idea (as well as being vanishingly unlikely). On the other hand, as perhaps the development of Japanese rating agencies demonstrates, there may be a useful role for government in sponsoring or encouraging new agencies suited to local conditions.[3]

Why a Social Foundations View Is Essential to Understanding Rating Agencies

Until the mid-1990s scholarly writing about the agencies was dominated by business school financial economists. This work typically sought to identify what was central to rating determination and what was not, to help the issuers of bonds secure a better rating and thus lower funding costs. What was common to this work and its contemporary equivalent is the idea that rating is, or should be, a technical matter, like automobile assembly or a root canal. Underlying this expectation was the assumption that there are cor-

---

2. Paul R. La Monica, "Elizabeth Warren Wants the SEC to Crack Down on Moody's and S&P," *CNN Business*, September 27, 2019, available at https://edition.cnn.com/2019/09/27/investing/elizabeth-warren-sec-ratings-agencies/index.html, accessed December 8, 2019.

3. Fumihito Gotoh and Timothy J. Sinclair, "Social Norms Strike Back: Why American Financial Practices Failed in Japan." *Review of International Political Economy* 24, no. 6 (2017): 1030–1051.

rect and incorrect ways to do rating, just as there are correct and incorrect ways to install spark plugs or swim backstroke.

It would be good if things were as simple as this. But it turns out that trying to understand rating this way is of limited veracity. Unsurprisingly, following this line, authorities have made little progress in addressing the rating enigma. The approach taken by most people to understanding rating is synchronic. This mentality, which is about solving problems, focuses on the properties of the system. Such an approach makes sense when the properties are fixed, such as they are in, say, an automobile engine. The synchronic approach is a sensible one for many practical problems in this world. For designing apartment buildings and food mixers, thinking about the properties of a system as fixed makes sense most of the time.

A different approach is required for thinking about institutions in the social world because social life is much more dynamic than nature. The diachronic approach suggests that understanding the properties of a system like a specific institution is just the first step to obtaining a full picture. We also need to understand the potential for change inherent in the institution. This suggests a longer-term, organic approach that appreciates that change may go in different directions, given different circumstances. The future is not fixed by the properties of the system, although these characteristics may make some outcomes more likely than others.

In addition to adopting this more historical and evolutionary way of thinking about the agencies, which helps to explain their adaptability and longevity, we also need to adopt what I call a social foundations approach. The essence of this way of thinking can be found in Keynes's "beauty contest metaphor." Keynes argued that people in the financial markets do not think about the fundamental merits of an investment in isolation. They are, instead, focused on outdoing their rivals in the markets. Since Keynes's time the calculative techniques deployed to make money via financial speculation have developed greatly. Confidence in these tools of calculation "as ostensibly scientific, legitimate and [as] more than mere speculation" is an important dimension of the social foundations approach.[4]

Collective thinking, including calculative techniques, is fundamental to the rating product. The agencies have no tangible product, unlike a steelmaker or even a bank. All they have is an intangible reputation for good judgment. While in certain circumstances ratings have been mandated by the US government and other governments around the world, Moody's, S&P, and Fitch have the majority of the rating market because other agencies do not have the hold on collective thinking these three global agencies enjoy. Some rating agencies are important. Most are not.

Financial Innovation Creates Problems

Starting in 2007, and for years afterward, discussions of what became known as the global financial crisis revolved around new securities referred to collectively as structured finance. Structured finance is not intuitive, like a bond or a loan. When a corporation issues a bond, that corporation may go bankrupt if it fails to repay bondholders, who then have recourse to all the assets of the company. This is not how structured finance works, because trusts intermediate the process of raising capital between borrowers and lenders. Lenders do not have recourse to the assets of the company behind the fund should the fund fail.

On top of this, a whole new world of derivative products developed to insure these trusts, allowing traders to make money by buy-

---

4. Email from Paul Langley to the author, January 8, 2019.

ing and selling these derivatives in secondary markets. Later, when the financial crisis was in full swing, the conceptual and substantive challenges of structured finance meant that when bankers, especially senior managers, were asked about these financial instruments they were sometimes unable to give convincing answers about how they worked. Many observers blamed structured finance for the crisis.

Like bonds, structured finance is a promise to repay the lender or investor. The major motivation to raise money by selling structured securities rather than ordinary bonds is to reduce the cost of borrowing to the issuer. Lower costs follow from establishing a pool of diversified assets with greater cash flow certainty than the credit of a single company. This means the pool will attract stronger credit ratings, allowing issuers to pay less to investors than they would otherwise when they sell them structured finance instruments such as collateralized debt obligations (CDOs). A structure of protection is crafted, based on anticipated losses over time, giving different rights to streams of income, based on diverging appetites for risk among investors. Compare this with debt securities from emerging markets where the risk of loss may be uncertain and impossible to calculate.

A key phenomenon, missed by most observers at the time of the crisis, has come into sharper focus in recent appraisals. This is the role of repurchase agreements, or repo, in magnifying the escalating market uncertainty in 2007 and 2008 into a truly massive event with global ramifications. Structured finance was not itself ground zero for the global financial crisis, despite the many thousands of words that have been written about this financial innovation. The thing that tore everything up, that caused the panic, was the use of structured finance in the repo markets, the "true heart" of the global financial crisis. Traditionally, the repo markets have put a premium on very high quality collateral to secure those loans, and the collateral of choice has been US Treasuries, because of their unmatched credit quality. But as the repo markets developed, other securities, including structured financings, were used as collateral. Repo was gigantic, with trillions of dollars in collateral posted on a daily basis just prior to the Lehman collapse. It also proved to be very fragile once panic set in and it no longer behaved according to expectations.

Is Rating Different Now?

In talking to rating agency officials since the start of the global financial crisis, I have observed their exasperation at the constant allegations of malfeasance directed at them. This was tinged with fatalism, as it became clear that no amount of testimony would absolve the organizations from the public proclamation of their guilt made by others. As Harrington's epigram at the start of chapter 7 indicates, exasperation and fatalism turned into a dogged determination to do their job, with the expectation they would be vilified whatever they did. This is not a unique situation. Other professionals face these sorts of difficulties. Think of probation officials (or, indeed, any part of the criminal justice system), corporate lawyers and tax accountants everywhere, aesthetic plastic surgeons, and political party organizers. None of them can win, and they know it.

The agencies face much higher compliance costs as they seek to generate the information required by SEC and ESMA and to implement new internal checks and quality controls. It helps, of course, that these businesses have some of the highest profit margins obtainable. The impression I have, as I have sometimes when considering my own professional context, is that all of this has been enervating, and destructive of real substantive acuity in what these organizations do and the contribution they make to the investment process. When you impose many new regulative rules on an activity but do not penetrate to the heart of that sector's constitutive rules with a constructive purpose, the outcome is not going to be effective. This leads to endless "firefighting" by the professionals involved. That is the situation we are in with rating.

I would like at this point to be able to conclude that the agencies have reverted to rating's diachronic roots as a check on shorttermism and speculative excess in global finance. That is, after all, why rating was so successful quickly after the 1907 financial crash. It offered an informed but very different way of thinking about finance, the utility of which was obvious. It is the case that the synchronic approach to rating that took root with the growth of structured finance, which only active participation by the agencies could make possible, has not been extinguished.[5]

What We Want from Rating—and What We Should Want

More than a decade on from the major events of the global financial crisis, many people remain dissatisfied with the major rating agencies. People seem to want much greater certainty about the future than the rating agencies offer. Ron Grassi's likening of rating to a report card is telling. Report cards list student grades, which is information about past performance. Ratings are predictions about the future, based on the track record (or report card) of the securities issuer and estimations of the challenges ahead. It seems people do not accept the uncertainty associated

---

5. Cezary Podkul and Gunjan Banerji, "Inflated Bond Ratings Helped Spur the Financial Crisis. They're Back," *Wall Street Journal*, August 7, 2019, https://www.wsj.com/articles/inflated-bond-ratings-helped-spur-the-financial-crisis-theyre-back-11565194951?mod=article_inline, accessed December 8, 2019.

with rating, thinking it should somehow be as reliable as information about the past.

Behind this view of the agencies are ideas about how the financial markets work. Finance is understood as being like a machine, or like the movements of planets in the cosmos. This view of the financial markets is closely linked to the exogenous account of financial crises I discussed in chapter 7. The rating agencies, although not financial institutions themselves, are drawn into this view of what finance is and how it works.

If people want certainty, they will continue to be unhappy about what rating can achieve. Rating, like all thinking about the future, is inevitably speculative in nature, no matter how we tinker with the analytic models. Ratings are similar to speech, in that the identity of the speaker matters. Some speakers are more authoritative than others. This means that some rating agencies—the Big Three—have more epistemic authority than the others. Eliminating the NRSRO category in the United States would not change this picture significantly. But one step to improving the public understanding of rating would be to eliminate NRSRO recognition, lowering the barriers to entry into the rating market.[6] This will not make rating disappear. But in time, people would at least not be able to blame government for the use of ratings and might become more judicious about using them.[7] It might actually encourage a wider view of the agencies with more in common with the social foundations approach I have advocated in this book.

---

6. For a good discussion of removal of the NRSRO designation, see Richardson et al., "Credit Rating Agencies and the Financial CHOICE Act," 173–178.

7. Cheryl Evans, "What Makes You So Special? Ending the Credit Rating Agencies' Special Status and Access to Confidential Information," *Valparaiso Law Review* 46, no. 4 (2012): 1091–1137.

We can, of course, continue to adjust government interventions into rating in the United States and Europe. This is the work of the SEC and ESMA. This work, focusing on transparency and competition, has had limited impact so far and is likely to offer similarly modest gains in future for the reasons I discussed in chapter 6. Focusing on regulative rules, rules that regulate a preexisting system, can only ever really amount to modest adjustments. More ambitious efforts, such as changing the compensation models for rating, or challenging analytical models, step beyond where most policymakers wish to go. A step in the right direction would require rating agencies to show they behave more like police patrols and less like fire alarms, seeking out evidence of financial stress and stopping the problems at their inception.[8]

I embrace a traditional diachronic and countercyclical view of ratings' purpose. If we look back to the 1920s when rating had only just emerged from the record-keeping about railroad bonds begun by of Henry Varnum Poor, and became a market expectation, free of government usage and regulation, I think we have the best model of what rating can provide. We could build on Ron Grassi's mistaken analogy with report cards. I suspect this would need to come from the agencies themselves given the reluctance of governments to tell the agencies what business they are in. The agencies could agree to publicly abandon trying to predict the future and instead focus on the *historical record of the issuer.* This would leave investors to work out for themselves whether they wish to take a chance on an issuer in the future, based only on their historical record of repaying. Ratings of this type—let us call them "historical ratings"

---

8. Matthew D. McCubbins and Thomas Schwartz, "Congressional Oversight Overlooked: Police Patrols versus Fire Alarms," in *Congress: Structure and Policy*, ed. Matthew D. McCubbins and Terry Sullivan (New York: Cambridge University Press, 1987).

or something similar—would not work for structured finance, because the differences in ratings between the tranches are crucial. But perhaps that is a good thing.

Researching Rating

Research on the rating agencies has grown significantly since the mid-1990s when rating actions started to impact on rich countries like Australia and Canada. Enron, the global financial crisis, and the European sovereign debt crisis have greatly highlighted the role of the agencies since then. Given concerns raised about the rating agencies' business model and the rating process itself, we should expect to see scholars and researchers undertake more work on these issues in future. But given the analysis presented in this book, I am not confident new work in this area will produce either a substantial contribution to knowledge or changes in practice if it adopts the market-centered approach to understanding the agencies.

I am an advocate of research in two areas. The first is investigating the spread of rating geographically and functionally. The growth of rating in emerging market societies is interesting because people do things in different ways across cultures. At present, and for the time being, these new rating agencies do not matter. They pose no threat to the market share of the Big Three, and they are unlikely to for years to come. But like the growth of China, things can change fast sometimes. So, research in this area must be very forward focused, looking at new approaches and methods that might, in the right circumstances, start to displace the Big Three. We do not know what that will be, but we need to be ready when it starts to happen. In addition to this focus on geography we need to consider the tendency of rating to creep into other functions, to subject these too to codified expectations about the future.

The second area I think worth pursuing is investigating why people have such inflated views about what rating can achieve. The idea that rating can tell you what will happen in the future is, I suspect, tied up with the continued dominance of the exogenous view of finance and financial crises I discussed in chapter 7. These ideas, which seem utopian to me, are perverse given the reality of uncertainty in predicting the future, especially in the case of financial innovation. In prior work, in this book, and in my work with Mennillo, I have explored some of the dynamics of authority and dominance enjoyed by the Big Three. Ironically, as risk has become less socialized for most inhabitants of the rich countries during the last thirty years, for example in the move from defined-benefit to defined-contribution pensions, individuals have become more dependent than ever on rating, even as its limits have become clearer. It seems we have fallen back on the idea that intellectual tools like rating can—and must—save us from an indeterminate future. Given what I found in writing this book this seems like a dangerous trend to me.

The Rating Enigma

Rating agencies seem to offer us a lot. This makes them very attractive. The idea that we can peer into an uncertain future is intoxicating. We do not read or take notice of the fine print that says ratings should only be part of the investment decision-making process. The rise of the agencies follows a great fall and a near-death experience. But it is clear few really have a good understanding of what rating can really offer. Many more in government and in the markets want rating to offer more than it can, and are surprised and disappointed when ratings fail, as they do again and again. What they are unwilling to accept as revealed by financial history is that finance itself is prone to boom and bust, and that no amount of analysis of likely future scenarios, which is all rating can offer, is ever likely to eliminate this pattern. That is the main story about financial crisis. The rating agencies are downstream actors in the process. But to recognize these endogenous problems, that finance is not a simple machine, but frequently runs out of control, a social institution in its own right, seems more than most are willing to accept given how challenging such a realization is to the way we have organized our societies.

The real problem with excessively heightened expectations of the rating agencies occurs in bull markets, when conditions are euphoric, and nothing seems to be impossible. As we have seen, in these times, given the pressure to keep business, utopian ideas about what ratings can achieve get transferred from outside the agencies into their inner workings. At this point, almost anything is possible.

Smart people in key institutions like rating agencies, banks, pharmaceutical companies, core public agencies, and perhaps even universities and research institutions recognize these pressures in their own work. They engage in developing strategies to reduce expectations and manage the quality of what they do every day. As this book shows, these efforts do not always work. The rating enigma—driven by these pressures in the broader context of the volatile, uncertain world of global finance—is likely to continue for years to come.

Index

.

Lightning Source UK Ltd.
Milton Keynes UK
UKHW011821270122
397772UK00004B/107/J

9 781501 760242